FINALE

FINALE

LATE INTERVIEWS WITH STEPHEN SONDHEIM

D. T. Max

HARPER

An Imprint of HarperCollins*Publishers*

HarperCollins books may be purchased for educational, business,
or sales promotional use. For information, please email the Special
Markets Department at SPsales@harpercollins.com.

Portions of this book appeared in slightly different form in
the *New Yorker* and at newyorker.com.

FIRST EDITION

Designed by Bonni Leon-Berman

Library of Congress Cataloging-in-Publication Data has been
applied for.

ISBN 978-0-06-327981-0

22 23 24 25 26 LSC 10 9 8 7 6 5 4 3 2 1

To my parents, Herbert and Dorothy,
who first brought me music

CONTENTS

FINALE

PRELUDE

I always wanted to write about Stephen Sondheim. Actually, long before writing about him was a possibility, I just wanted to meet Stephen Sondheim. In the spring of that long-ago year 1977, my mother went to a benefit for the Phoenix Theatre, a repertory company that pioneered off-Broadway theater. The event included a performance of *Side by Side by Sondheim*, a revue of the composer-lyricist's songs. Going to benefits was not the sort of thing my mother usually did, but my uncle was a playwright whom the Phoenix had championed, and he might have persuaded her. Sondheim at the time was exactly the sort of creator the Phoenix wanted to associate itself with. He was remaking the American musical in the same way the Phoenix was trying to remake the theatrical landscape.

In 1977, I was fifteen. As part of the benefit package, my mother came home with a two-record album of the show. It was signed by Hal Prince, the artistic director of the Phoenix, in Magic Marker, and below that was Sondheim's signature, in a more delicate hand, his S's like two treble clefs. I had never seen a signed book or album, hadn't even known people did that. On the album cover, Sondheim, in profile—bearded, dark brow lowered—glared off into space. Behind him hovered the logos for his many musicals: *West Side Story, Gypsy, A Funny Thing Happened on the Way to the Forum, Anyone Can Whistle, Do I Hear a Waltz?, Company, Follies, A Little Night Music,* and *Pacific Overtures.* Nine amazing shows—and he was still only in his mid-forties. His imposing body language—chin up, arms crossed—seemed to promise more were on the way.

My family lived in a large Upper West Side apartment. My parents agreed on very little, and so many rooms had almost no furniture, but in our living room there stood a gorgeous walnut-paneled KLH Model Twenty-Plus stereo my mother had bought and my father had paid for. The fight over its price had exceeded the hi-fi's top volume, but that had been many years before. By now it had settled into place along one wall, near the ornate fireplace with layers of landlord paint covering the plaster putti.

My father, a lawyer, would put Dave Brubeck's "Take Five," a favorite of his, on the spindle, slide the lever, and down the disc would drop with a click. Despite a warning in the stereo manual not to, if you pulled the throw-arm to the side, a record would play over and over—and that's what my father did. He worked away on legal matters as the record spun around and around. He was the only one in the family who could whistle, and sometimes from the back of the apartment where my brothers and I dwelt, I could hear Brubeck and him in a duet.

In 1976, I bought a copy of *A Chorus Line* after seeing the musical. The show immediately spoke to me—the harsh judging, the self-doubt, the final triumph. The songs were memorable—"I Hope I Get It," "What I Did for Love"—and

I loved them. Soon my father was playing them, too. Back went the throw-arm, down plopped *A Chorus Line* on top of Brubeck. "One! Singular sensation!" He even whistled the songs.

Every once in a while, my mother—or was it me?—would put one of the two *Side by Side by Sondheim* records on the spindle and let it drop. Songs with names like "You Must Meet My Wife," "Being Alive," and "Another Hundred People" would play then in the living room, spinning on top of the gyrating pile. These were witty, intricate, self-conscious tunes that got at life not through the front door but through a side window in a way that was new to me.

> . . . *Another hundred people who got off of the plane*
> *And are looking at us*
> *who got off of the train.*

I soon understood that Sondheim's songs were special in ways those from *A Chorus Line* were not. True, they weren't as easily singable and definitely not as whistleable. Nor did his characters sing to express overwhelming emotions or resolve simple doubts the way Cassie and Diana did in *A Chorus Line*. Instead, Sondheim's characters were made of doubt, of missteps, of ambivalence. Marry me a little. Side by side . . . by side. This complexity extended to the music itself, which Sondheim filled with tricky rhythms and harmonic improbabilities. Soon the songs in *A Chorus Line* seemed overbright to me, trying too hard to win my affection.

The liner notes for *Side by Side by Sondheim* suggested that *Company* had not been a success at first in its London run in

1972 because it was too New York for Londoners, and added cleverly that the same had been true of the original Broadway show two years earlier—that it was, in fact, almost too New York for New Yorkers. The musical revolves around a quintet of couples trying to persuade their single friend Bobby to commit despite their own mixed feelings about marriage. That group of arch, insecure, promiscuous frenemies—could that have been life there then? Even in my mid-teens, I knew it was. Sondheim's music captured perfectly the New York I grew up in, with its graffitied subways and pot-filled parties, its uncertain adults and its adult children. By comparison, *A Chorus Line* often felt to me like just an out-of-towner's idea of Manhattan.

Over the next four decades, I never got over my sense of having a unique connection to Sondheim, that he was, in some way, writing to me. In high school, I was in a production of *West Side Story* (in a nonsinging part, luckily for the audience). In my late-teens, twenties, and thirties, I saw his shows whenever they were performed—*Sweeney Todd* and *Passion*, and revivals of *Merrily We Roll Along* and *Company*. My thirties also included a CD of *Assassins* that I listened to over and over. Through all those years, he was the only living show composer whose work I cared about—even the only one I could name. But it's also true that I did many other things. I went to college, graduated, went to work, met my wife, had two children, had a dog that grew old and died, became a writer and wrote two books as well as profiles of lots of people who did lots of remarkable things—a chef, a neuroscientist, a curator, a pianist, a chess champion, an environmentalist, and a passel of novelists. Each interested me fiercely in turn. Otherwise I could not have written about them. Still, I never forgot Sondheim or the album with his gracile signature.

Then, in late 2016, I saw Sondheim's name on a list of prospective profile subjects at the *New Yorker*, where I was now a staff writer. According to the memo, the composer and lyricist had a new musical coming out based on two movies—one from the 1960s, the other from the '70s—by the surrealist director Luis Buñuel. This sounded too good to be true. *Company* had marked the start of an amazing, nearly twenty-five-year run that included *Follies*, *Pacific Overtures*, *Sweeney Todd*, through to *Sunday in the Park with George*, *Into the Woods*, and *Passion*. But by the late 2000s, Sondheim's productivity seemed to have diminished. He had spent years working on a musical titled, at various points, *Gold!*, *Wise Guys*, *Bounce*, and finally *Road Show*. The work, about a pair of con men brothers, had never achieved optimal form or made a Sondheim-level impression on audiences—and that had been nearly ten years ago. Silence since. It was fair to ask if Sondheim had finally lost his creative spark. He himself had said that composers always do their best work by fifty, and he, by then, was well into his eighties. In more recent years, so far as I knew, he had seemed to concern himself more with his legacy—revivals, retrospectives, and tributes—than with new shows.

To write a musical based on *The Exterminating Angel* and *The Discreet Charm of the Bourgeoisie*, as the snippet stated, was a step forward—and back, potentially, into classic Sondheim, which is to say into difficult, daring musicals. Although both films have bright, easy-to-dramatize setups—in *Discreet Charm* a group of bourgeois French couples are trying in vain to eat a meal together, while in *The Exterminating Angel*, similarly affluent couples are stuck at a party from which, for obscure reasons, they can't leave—neither has much in the way of character or plot. The difficulties the characters find themselves in are born out of class antagonisms rather than personalities—Buñuel wants to show how the bourgeoisie portend their own annihilation, a sentiment that seemed a hard fit with Sondheim, who was never doctrinaire.

Sondheim was known for never repeating himself, neither at the level of subject nor musical passage, and here clearly was more new ground to try to break. But could he do it? Could he *still* do it? I didn't know. I could imagine a result as innovative and delightful as *A Little Night Music*, his 1973 musical lightly inspired by the film *Smiles of a Summer Night*, or as ineluctably earthbound as the project Sondheim and Leonard Bernstein had worked on and abandoned after *West Side Story* in the 1960s, *A Pray by Blecht*, which, at least at one point, was a play within a play set in a television station and designed to show the meaninglessness of good intentions.

For me, the opportunity to see what was going on firsthand, and meet the genius I'd first encountered as a teen, was obviously appealing. But I wasn't sure how much fun it would be. To the extent I knew anything about Sondheim's public persona, his reputation was that of someone who guarded his privacy carefully. In 1998, when he was nearly seventy, the fact that he had spoken straightforwardly about his homosexuality in a just-published biography was treated as a revelation.

I could see why he might be mistrustful of the press. Even into the 1990s, many serious critics, including some who admired his aesthetic goals, had mixed feelings about his work. Some thought his music was more ambitious than successful. His songs were ungainly or overly clever and lacked hummable tunes. They were too arcane to be popular entertainment but not elevated enough to be art. A traditional musical left you enlarged by the magical world that had enfolded you. A Sondheim musical left you admiring the creator behind the music and words. "It's the triumph of the artist over the art," complained one critic in *Slate* in 1997, "the man who knows more than anyone else about musicals except how to write one where you don't notice how much he knows."

In fact, for a career that by 2016 was thought of as a unique triumph, Sondheim's progress had had fewer triumphant moments than one might imagine. It was really only when he stopped producing great work that what he had accomplished began to get its due. Works that today sound inarguably great and are regularly revived, like *Pacific Overtures*, which uses Asian musical tonalities to tell the story of the Western incursion into Japan, or *Sunday in the Park with George*, the story of the painter Seurat followed, in the second act, by the travails of a modern avant-garde artist, in their day came in for piñata-level attacks. Clive Barnes—the longtime theater critic of the *New York Times* but by then relegated to the *New York Post*—wrote of *Sunday in the Park* when it opened in 1984, that he was "nonplussed, unplussed, and disappointed," criticizing the play for "a somewhat simplistic and bathetically pretentious course in art appreciation." Robert Brustein, in the *New*

Republic, wrote that "Sondheim, once again frowning on melody, is here composing in a minimalist, vaguely serial style which functions primarily as a setting for his surprising, often witty lyrics."

In the end, of course, Sondheim outlasted his critics. It didn't hurt that the demise of print media winnowed his opposition as efficiently as Sweeney's barber chair. But that was just chance. More importantly, a new generation grew up who embraced his work without reserve. The movies, TV shows, and books they loved were also more oblique and knowing, closer to the act of thinking than performing. Sondheim's lyrics and music fit into the world as they knew it. To them, everything before Sondheim in musical theater was dated, and those works created in their own time, if they were any good, owed an obvious debt to him. As Lin-Manuel Miranda said a couple of months after Sondheim's death in November of 2021, "Anyone who tells you that Sondheim isn't an influence on their music or their work is lying."

But this was the triumphant end. The trip through the woods had surely taken its toll. Maybe no one is alone but that doesn't mean you don't feel that way. Over time, Sondheim had developed a public persona that was brassy and comic. He was often available to the press, especially if a show was about to open, without really being open. He was happy to talk, but he often kept things impersonal.

Still, in 2016, a brilliant musical about the striving of the rich to protect themselves from the poor would have real resonance, tapping into the surreal nature of our times, where a small percentage of people owned nearly all there was to own and any lie repeated enough could find believers. And it might finish an extraordinary career with one last outstanding achievement.

So I wrote an email to Sondheim's assistant to ask if the composer-lyricist was willing to be profiled. Not long afterward, Sondheim himself wrote back. That was a surprise. Most public figures of his stature don't respond—or, if they do, it is via a publicist, agent, or assistant. His note was plain, too, with none of the hauteur he was entitled to, nor the edge I presumed he contained. He began his response, "Dear Daniel (if I may)" and signed off "Yours, Steve S." Yes, he would be happy to sit for a portrait if I was interested.

Not that the note was without guile. I think it would have disappointed me if it had been. His brief email contained a fair amount of performance. First, he said it had taken him a few days to respond because he looked at email "only sporadically"—not really true, as I was to learn. He would turn out to be a pretty fast correspondent, a habit I suspected was connected inversely to how well his actual work was going. He added he would like to see something I'd written—not, he emphasized, as "an audition," but so we could talk more easily together. And he said he was flattered to be asked. That last just sounded ridiculous, given that he had by then won eight Tonys, eight Grammys, and a Presidential Medal of Freedom, and had a Broadway theater named after him.

Especially because he'd already been profiled in the *New Yorker*, in 1993, a fact I had forgotten and that he pointed out with nice delicacy, as if it were his fault I didn't remember. He implied later he had been disappointed in the first profile—he never said why—but that did not stop him from being game for another go-round.

I sent him a copy of a biography of David Foster Wallace I'd published a few years before and followed up about a week later to see if he'd gotten it. He responded soon after that the first sentence in my book, "Every story has a beginning and this is David Wallace's," reminded him of a first sentence he had just read in a memoir in that week's *New Yorker*: "Every love story has to start somewhere, and I'm blaming this one on a boat." He did not say in either case if he got beyond that sentence or liked the rest, though he said he could tell I was a serious writer. When I offered a date after the holidays, he accepted. I supposed I had passed the audition.

As I got ready for my first interview with Sondheim, I realized that, despite my decades of admiring his work, I could not recall even the most rudimentary things about him. I did not know where he was born, where he grew up, how he began in musical theater, who his friends were, or where he lived. I did not know what he looked like now that he was an old man or how he spoke. I did not know if he composed on a piano or in the bathtub, which of his musicals he loved best or whether the words came first or the music (I did remember one of the characters in *Merrily We Roll Along* answering that question with the reply, "the contract"). I did not know whether he was sorry he had no children or, as seemed more likely to me, he regarded his musicals as his offspring. I did not know if he had siblings or a partner or an ex. Hobbies? Pets? Vacation homes? Secrets? Although I had read or heard him interviewed from time to time over the years—it would have been hard to avoid it—it was curious how little of what I'd learned had seeped into my head, which suggested that, despite plenty of opportunity to reveal himself, some part of Sondheim remained offstage. The fact that musicals are collaborative—Sondheim wrote the songs and music in response to someone else's story—likely worked against a certain kind of insight too.

I thought about my ignorance and asked myself if it would irritate him, but I didn't think so. I thought Sondheim would like that, despite my obliviousness, he had changed my life. I would explain that there were three or four songs of his that were so familiar to me I couldn't remember when I'd first heard them. On dates in high school I would hum "Oh moon, grow bright," the lyric he composed to Leonard Bernstein's much crooned love tune from *West Side Story*. Leaving my native New York City with my then-girlfriend at the end of 2000 as we drove south to DC, I mournfully sang, "And every day some go away." And later, when we were married, "You must meet my wife" kept popping out of my mouth with some of the attendant comic bits. "She twitters. My word! Isn't that alarming? What is she, a bird?" I wasn't a critic. I wasn't a maven. I was just a listener.

On a practical level, my lack of expertise on Sondheim might turn out to work to my advantage. The cliché that chance favors the prepared mind sometimes applies to interviewing but not always. In fact, the opposite can be true, especially in an era where information is so easy to get hold of. The best way to prepare is sometimes not to: to prepare only to be off-balance, often corrected, and occasionally embarrassed. Here's why: first, most people whom you want to interview, if they agree to sit down with you, want to communicate what they have done. They are trying to shape the story in your mind. They are also, by nature or accomplishment, teachers. And it's their words, expressing their experience, you want most of all, not your own. They also often have egos. If you come to them exuding expertise as to the details of their life or work, you risk provoking their competitiveness. One thing I strongly suspected from his stance on the *Side by Side by Sondheim* album cover was that Sondheim wasn't waiting for any critiques that I might have to offer. He would want to be in control of the discussion, the goal of which was to tutor me.

Another potential problem was that Sondheim had been interviewed what seems like hundreds of times, well and badly, and likely had by now developed a quasi-formula to respond to questions, many of which he had heard before. People who are interviewed often settle on a shtick, a way to just get through it. I hoped I would be able to push him just far enough out of his routine to get a fresh glimpse of who he was. To do this, I wasn't going to try to impress him. It might be nice that I liked puzzles and rhymes, as I knew he did—but he had, I presumed, access to the conversation of the most remarkable people on the planet. Any idea, any person, any experience was within his reach. What I trusted in was that the overall thrust of his work, for all its caveats about other people—their waning sex appeal, their bodily emanations, their repetitious opinions—was toward human companionship. Life is company. He might still enjoy someone wanting his. He might even be lonely. He was in his late eighties, after all, and had already outlived nearly everyone he knew. I thought of a story about Mark Twain that

I had run into in the course of researching a new book. As an old man, Twain had desperately sought the attention of young people he could amuse. Once, on an Atlantic crossing, the steward had had to intercede with a young woman who had grown tired of his patter: "It's a shame to keep the old man waiting like that," he lectured her. Such things happened.

All these thoughts were just guesses, and doubtless they left a lot out. In the end, I would just try to have a conversation, much like two people who happen to sit next to each other on a flight and don't quickly come to wish it was shorter, or who are seated together at a wedding because the marrying couple thought they might have something in common. I wanted what took place between us to be humble, unremarkable, non-interview-y. That meant come often, don't stay too long, don't be too intense, take some breaks to fill up at the buffet. My hope was that I might catch Sondheim just a bit differently than anyone else had, good as some of those earlier interviews had been. And from there I would construct a profile, an interpretation. One thing I had in my favor was that he was old now. Coming to the end, to state it plainly. It might be a time of openness for him. He'd be familiar, of course—how could he not be?—but it was possible too, that in this most reflective time of life, he might come out a bit more nuanced, more complex, more Sondheimian.

AUDITION

JANUARY 2016

"The danger is you would be in on all the difficult decisions."

So one day in January 2017, I stood in front of a series of low connected houses in the East 40s. The word "maisonette" was going through my head. What were the possible rhymes? Red Corvette? Press-Gazette? Raisinet? It was January but mild. Evening. Pink sunset? I walked down a few stairs and rang an unmarked doorbell. Phone rings, door chimes, and in went me—directly into a living room like an old stage set. A member of the house staff ushered me in, and down from staircase stage left descended Sondheim. He was a bit stooped, but moved fast, without the lag the elderly often have. Two dogs, which he'd mentioned in an email, were racing around. One, Sondheim had told me, loved food, the other loved people, but, as often happens with other people's dogs, I couldn't tell any difference. The composer sat and from various unidentified doors and staircases staff and friends wandered through—some to say something to him, others just to go in and out other doors, yet others to groom Willie (or maybe it was Addie) or serve the wine. Sondheim talked to all, the lead, humorous, sardonic, and appealing, beloved but not lovable, in the Shavian way. The decor was imposing, maybe frozen. Items of obvious interest—some behind museum-level glass—dotted the room: little wooden structures, antique games, obscure gadgetry. My guess was each had a story, and many probably led to Mary Rodgers or Oscar Hammerstein.

We first made some small talk about dogs, including the fact that my beagle, who came to my family already named Max, had died several years before. Sondheim surprised me with the news that he too had had a dog named Max who had died in a fire in the house twenty-five-years before that had also damaged his archives. It was hard to know what he felt when he told me things like this. He had a loud, *Guys & Dolls*-y voice, the growl of a former smoker. In affect he was still the forty-five-year-old from my old album cover, unbowed before the withering critics, but in appearance he now looked more like a kibitzer, the kind of guy who could give good commentary from under an umbrella by the side of the tennis court. His left eye was nearly closed, as if he was in the middle of a wink. This gave everything he said, no matter how serious, the appearance at first of a joke. I would have to get past that impression, I reminded myself, to hear what he was saying.

My need to come in from Jersey I had always found to be a good conversational opener—encompassing questions of class and traffic, those American icebreakers, and rendering me, usually, a sympathetic applicant. So after the dog discussion, I asked him where he was from, and we began to talk. I began by asking:

Are you a New Jersey person by ancestry?

Oh, not at all.

Because my people are.

Oh yeah? I was born right in the middle of Manhattan.

You were?

Yes, exactly—at a hospital that no longer exists, called Women's Hospital. I once took a map of Manhattan and marked the northernmost, westernmost, easternmost, and southernmost apartments and houses I had been in, and I drew it out, and I cut out Central Park, and I've lived my entire life in twenty square blocks.

Wow.

You wanna talk about parochial!

I didn't realize that. There's an E. B. White essay about how the people who really enjoy Manhattan are the ones who come to it, and for some reason I thought you were among them.

Great essay. You know where he used to live?

No, where did he live? On this street?

About a hundred feet. [*He points south, happily.*] There! On the other side of the community garden, the Turtle Bay Gardens. There are twenty houses: ten on this side, ten on 48th. He lived on the 48th Street side, and he used to write in the

New Yorker a column called a Letter from the East, and "the East" meant the East Side. And that tree that is mentioned in the essay—it was cut down four years ago because finally it fell apart, but it was out there.

I didn't realize that. I read that essay years ago, and I always thought it didn't involve me, because I was born here.

In Manhattan?

Yeah, I was born in Manhattan, too.

You're maybe the third person I've met in my entire life who can say that.

But I grew up on the Upper West Side.

That's where I grew up! Well, on 75th Street.

Yeah, I grew up on 89th. You're 75th and what?

The first twelve years of my life, the San Remo. Ten years. Then my parents got divorced, and my father moved to the East Side, and blah, blah. But the first ten years, I went to Ethical Culture. Fieldston. Where'd you go?

[I name another progressive day school, which he has never heard of. I tell him about it and he's interested and asks questions.]

In my day, Ethical Culture was the school.

The private schools when I was young were desirable, but they were desirable schools in a dying city. Now you feel the force of wanting at the doors like nothing I've ever known.

To get in now?

Yeah. So, where'd you go to high school?

When my parents got divorced, my mother got custody of me, and she bought a so-called farm in Doylestown, Pennsylvania.

Oh, wow.

Which is about an hour and a half away.

Bucks County?

Yeah, Bucks County. It's *just* across the border. So, there's this school nearby called George School, which was and is a Friends school. It's a Quaker school, but it's not orthodox Quaker. It was co-ed, and it's an old school—founded in 1890. And I went to boarding school there for four years.

Oh, you went to boarding school?

George was a boarding school. My mother was a workingwoman, and my father by that time had remarried and lived in Stamford, Connecticut, so I couldn't have gone to a day school, and I didn't want to.

And your father paid the tuition?

Well, he did, but my mother was a case, to put it mildly. My mother was a classic case of—it was not good. She was not interested in being a mother. She was interested in her career. She didn't want me in the first place, so it was to her taste to get rid of me—and to my taste to get rid of her. And we lived three miles from Oscar Hammerstein, and my mother was a celebrity . . . a celebrity-fucker, was what I was going to say.

I mean, she just loved celebrities and money. Those were her two mainstays.

But she was in Doylestown. And Oscar Hammerstein—
Was also in Doylestown. Three miles away. And they had a son my age, so we became friends, and Oscar became my surrogate father. They saved my life emotionally, because my mother was difficult.

[The pause that follows encourages me to change the subject. I bring up all the revivals of Sondheim's musicals that are about to open in New York.]

I saw that there was a revival of *Sunday in the Park*, I think it was—
Yeah, that's coming up.

And when is that?
Do you know the City Center Encores series?

Yeah, of course I do.
OK, well, Jeanine Tesori started a summer encore series, and they did this one a few months ago starring Jake Gyllenhaal, and it worked out well, and he wanted to transfer it. So it's now going to reopen the Hudson Theatre, which used to be a theater and then became a radio theater.

I think I know where that is.
It's on 44th, just east of Broadway. If you ever go to any show from the East Side, you pass the Hudson Theatre. And it's on the north side of 44th.

But that's just a revival.

That's just a revival.

I'm not sure we could hang a profile on that.

No, no, no. What's interesting—what you should see and what might be fun for your kids, too—is there's gonna be a revival of *Sweeney Todd*, which goes into rehearsal next week. It was done in London in a pie shop, not in the theater, while you eat. They are transforming the Barrow Street Theatre into a pie shop. In London, the oldest meat-pie shop is called Harrington's, and that's where it was done. The pie shop sat thirty people—the entire pie shop is probably the area of this room. And there were tables on this side, and the counter there, and all the acting was done right in your lap, so to speak. Anyway, Cameron Mackintosh saw it at my recommendation, and he transferred it to Shaftesbury Avenue, and transformed a theater into a pie shop. So here it's gonna be done—I mean, you'll eat meat pies. In London you ate eel pies.

Oh, God.

[*Laughs*] No, actually, they're very good!

Eel pies are?

Yeah, yeah, they're good!

What's the seasoning?

In eel? Oh, you're asking someone who doesn't know salt from pepper.

Oh, really?

Yeah.

I'm such an eater. I was on your block, and I was like oh, there's Indian food …

Oh, this neighborhood, within a five-block walk, there's virtually every ethnic food.

'Cause you're near the U.N. It's a happy location.

That's right.

[I turn to the subject of his new musical, based on the Buñuel films, and ask if it would be possible to watch a workshop or a rehearsal. Profiles usually benefit from people doing something besides talking. The subject reveals themself through their interactions with their world.]

I'll talk to Oskar Eustis, who runs the Public, and to Scott Rudin—they're the producers—and see what they think. I think they might go for it. But Scott is the definition of the word "volatile."

He's also a genius.

Yeah, that is true. He's also real smart. Very, very good at editing and criticizing and *judging* writing. He understands writing.

Years ago, I saw a movie of his called *Searching for Bobby Fischer*.

Oh, that's one of my favorites. I like that movie so much, it's the only time I ever wrote a fan letter to a screenwriter: Steven Zaillian. I got his address and I thought—I don't write fan letters very often, maybe four in my entire life, and that movie, *Searching for Bobby Fischer*, just knocked me out.

Yeah, I loved that movie. What was cool about it for me is that it's not a showy screenplay. So much is left to the acting. And yet the screenplay itself is an absolutely beautiful piece of writing in its own funny, elliptical way.

You're describing Chekhov. When you read Chekhov, you say, "This is a play? Come on! A lot of people are just chattering, and that's it? And then the curtain comes down? What happens? Is anything *happening*?" No—a dramatist *has* to write for actors. If you don't write for actors, and you spell everything out, and you avoid what they call subtext, you get a really boring play. As, I think, with movies. Hitchcock's a great example of what you don't show.

I've never been a Hitchcock guy.

What about *Shadow of a Doubt*? *Shadow of a Doubt* is about as good of a movie as—

I didn't even know he made a movie called *Shadow of a Doubt*.

Oh man, oh man, oh man.

[I turn back to the subject of his new musical.]

Anyway, if you talk to Oskar—

I'll talk to him. I think it might attract him a lot. And it certainly would be an unusual piece. It wouldn't be the first piece, but it would be unusual, particularly because most pieces about how shows are put together start when the rehearsals begin, as opposed to when it's still being developed.

Right. And for me, it's got to be good, and it's gotta be totally thought through. As a writer myself—

I can tell from what I've read of yours. That's what I meant when I said you were serious.

Thank you. I mean, you create a work of art. You do things that work, that don't work. And somebody who chronicles it doesn't go to score off it. It's creation. That's what makes it exciting. Who else is involved?

Oskar Eustis, and Scott, and Joe Mantello, who is as good a director as there is, so that's the—there's a terrible word that shows up in programs now.

What is it?

The creatives. There are the actors and then the *creatives*.

And the next step is a March reading?

At the moment, what's set is toward the end of March is a reading of, supposedly, a complete first act, and then as much of the second act as we can maneuver.

And then in theory it would arrive at the Public—

In theory, I think the idea is to do it in the spring of '18.

That certainly gives me time to warm up my pen.

Ha! It may be a little earlier, maybe the end of '17, but somewhere in there. I'll find out. I'll see what they say, and you see what your guys say. The danger is that you would be in on all the difficult decisions that may very well then color the reviewers. I'm just saying—I always look for the red flags.

So don't let me in on all of them.

You know what I'm saying.

I'm not—

I mean, you're a reporter.

You want to do your best, but I also recognize that there are moments where having a person like me in the room doesn't feel like the most natural thing. There are levels of privacy.

Oh, that wasn't what I was thinking. I was thinking, for example, we discuss, "Should we go with A, or should we go with B?" And then it shows on the stage, and we went with B, and someone who's read your piece says, "They should have gone with A."

I think the actual more delicate part is casting, because there are people who are chosen and people who are not chosen, and that gets awkward. But I'm much more interested in structure, creativity, what you guys are doing—

I think what we should concentrate on is how the show *reaches* this rehearsal stage.

And also, remember, I came originally for you.

You came for me as a writer.

Exactly. If you had a scene you felt wasn't working, and you cut ten lines from it, that would be something I would be deeply interested in.

Well, you know that's something—I don't know if you've read my books, but I wrote two books. I wrote a book called *Finishing the Hat*, and I bet I have an extra copy here. It's this big book, and it's all about what we're talking about. And the second one was called *Look, I Made a Hat*. The lines are quotes from songs I wrote. I spent a couple years writing them, and I have to say they were chosen as one of the ten best books of the year by the *Times*. I go through show by show and talk about how some decisions were reached. I also talk about my colleagues, and so on.

Well, if you have a copy—
I will. It's very heavy!

I drove. I'll stick it in the back.
Oh, OK, let me see. [*He calls up to his assistant, who appears at the top of the stairs.*] Do we have an extra copy of *Finishing the Hat*? Can you bring it down for Daniel, please?

[*Another member of the household staff appears from behind a swinging door and asks if we want more wine.*]

I'll have another quick glass.
Oh, sure.

As long as you are—I don't want to stay beyond my welcome—
OK, we'll take another one.

[*Another glass of wine comes.*]

Where in Connecticut are you?
Just over the border—it's called Roxbury.

I know Roxbury. I've been to Roxbury.

I wouldn't be surprised; there's a lot of literary folk.

Is that what it is?

Bill Styron lived there, and Pete [A. R.] Gurney lives there. Who else is around . . . ? Anyway, it's really nice.

Have you been there a long time?

No. Well, it was 1984, so I guess it is a long time. It's an unpretentious—it *was* a farmhouse, a turkey farm. [*He tells me he's resisting the obvious joke about showbiz and turkeys.*]

I was waiting for that joke!

It's very modest. Sixteen acres.

You have sixteen acres! What do you do with them?

Well, let's see if I can describe it. There's the road, and my house is there, with nine acres of woods and a little lawn—essentially woods and trees. And then across from that is a barn, which one of my oldest friends lives in. On that side there are seven acres, and they're essentially fields.

[*His assistant comes down and gives me copies of both Sondheim's books.*]

Thank you; this is beautiful.

Oh no, come on.

[*Returning to the subject, I ask . . .*]

What exactly attracted you to Buñuel?

Well, David [*He is speaking of David Ives, the playwright and his collaborator on the project.*] and I started on another thing, and then we dropped that because another show was being done that had a *vaguely* similar notion to it, and in getting to know each other and working with each other, we found we had similar tastes. And *I* had had this idea for the Buñuel for at least twenty-five years, and the idea was taking these two movies and making one movie the first half and the other movie the second half. And I mentioned it to him, and of course he knew both movies, and he thought it was a swell idea. So, it's an idea that I've *had* for a very long time and never did anything about.

I haven't seen *Discreet Charm* since—do you remember the New Yorker Theater on 89th and Broadway? That's where I saw the name first. I grew up directly opposite.

[*I reminisce about looking out my bedroom window as a boy and seeing the line for Bertolucci's* The Spider's Stratagem *wrap all the way around to West End Avenue.*]

I saw it at the New York Film Festival!

Oh, you did? I didn't realize the film festival was that far back.
Guess what the very first movie was at the New York Film Festival?

[*A game! Sondheim is playing a game, and I'm determined to outwit him.*]

I can try if you give me the year.

I wanna say '64? '65?

Alright, '64 or '65.

Not an American movie.

Not an American movie—alright, so, that's got to be . . . *Curious (Yellow)*. Am I close?

No. Guess what? Why would I say, "Guess what?"

Oh, 'cause it's something called *Guess What*.

No! What are we talking about?

[*Pretending to hazard another guess*] We were talking about Bertolucci, *Spider's Stratagem* . . .

What else were we talking about? What have we been talking about for forty-five minutes?

Oh, [*I fake a moment of cogitation.*] Buñuel!

Exactly.

'64–'65 would be too early for *Discreet Charm*, right? That's later—so what's in between?

The Exterminating Angel. It's what opened the film festival.

He had such a long, interesting career. It's almost two Buñuels—to think the same guy who made those early movies also made *Discreet Charm*.

But the high comedies, the social comedies were very late in his career. I mean, you could see elements of them . . . but *Spider's Stratagem*, I saw at the film festival.

Are you a big filmgoer?

Yeah, I grew up on movies. As a matter of fact, in my early twenties, I was going to be a contestant on *The $64,000 Question* on the subject of movies. The final test before I could be a contestant was to name ten movies directed by John Ford between *Stagecoach* and *The Searchers*, out of fourteen.

I love *The Searchers*.

That's on my list of overrated. I like to say to people, "What's the most overrated book? What's the most overrated movie?"

I love that movie! How can you not love that movie? I mean, it's a free country...

I didn't say I hated it!

What would your favorite John Ford be?

That's an interesting question. *Grapes of Wrath*.

We're just different.

I love Westerns! *The Searchers* has just been overpraised.

Yeah, but that's not his fault. You of all people should know that you can't control if people love something or not.

No, of course not. But if it's a B+ on my scale and it's an A+ on yours, that's all fine, you know.

It's also how you see John Ford's movies. His movies are movies you want to see in a movie theater, because you watch them on any other screen—

A lot of it has to do with spectacle, no question. John Ford does not do intimate movies. I'm not talking about scenery. I mean, *Grapes of Wrath* is not an intimate movie. It's a *character* movie.

So what's your most—

Overrated movie ever?

Yeah.

Vertigo.

It's funny, I was gonna say *I* think it's Hitchcock, but I thought you won't say it's Hitchcock, because you love Hitchcock.

Oh, I love *good* Hitchcock. *Shadow of a Doubt* is one of my top ten movies, and *Vertigo* is the most overrated piece of shit.

Is that because it's overpraised?

No, it's because nothing happens in it, and it's endless, and it's slow, and one more shot of James Stewart driving the car through the empty streets of San Francisco . . .

I feel that way about most of Hitchcock, but I'm also kind of weird. I tend to like the less-loved sibling.

That's slightly perverse; I know that.

It is. I can't help it! And with writers I'm the exact same way. With Steinbeck, if you put a gun to my head, I would not reread *Grapes of Wrath*. I would rather take the bullet.

I gotcha. I gotcha.

But if you gave me those late books, when he was probably an alcoholic, and it cost him so much just to get anything out . . . Why don't you read much?

I think it's partly because I was brought up exposed to movies, which, first of all, you don't have to do any work, and second, they go by fast. And that may be my attention-span problem. But to this day, it takes me about three times as long to read the *New York Times* as it does you.

But you do poke around.

I just am a very slow reader, and therefore I never got into the habit. And boy, I took every novel course at Williams College—which is where I went—on American novels, and European novels, and curiously enough, none of them really made me want to read another one. Except I took a six-week course on *Ulysses*, and I thought, "Ooh, well, this is different. *This* is different!" Because of course there's *Ulysses* and there's everything else. But I love *The Way of All Flesh*.

Samuel Butler?

Mm-hmm. I thought it was *screamingly* funny.

I haven't read it in years.

You know, I haven't either, but I thought, "Oh, this is working."

Funny as in "accidentally funny"?

No, no, witty! And then, the first half of *Light in August*. I thought, "OK, now I get it." It's weird, because obviously

I'm *really* interested in language, and I love style, and I love all of that. But what happens—and it's unfair—is, if in the second paragraph of a book I think a sentence is out of style, I think, "Oh, fuck this."

Really?

That kind of impatience.

Well, lyrics have to be so tight.

That's right, 'cause sixty words is your limit, so to speak.

It has to be "Flight 18"; it can't be "Flight 19."

Yeah, exactly. I'm used to that compression. When I *have* enjoyed a book, I enjoy the expansion, and I remember reading *The Caine Mutiny*, not in college but on an airplane, and it was much longer, but by page twenty, I got into what was happening. And I knew exactly what I was reading. I knew I was reading a high-class potboiler, but I got into it. And I used to read detective novels, because I like puzzles. But I just have trouble reading. And I have tried to train myself—I really did. I read *everything* that the college offered, and a few books got me. *A Passage to India* got me.

That's a beautiful book.

Wonderful!

Have you ever seen the manuscript? It was written with an unusual colored ink. It's physically very striking to look at.

Have you ever seen the Brontës' writing? Jesus. I've never read their books, but I went to the Morgan—

If you're in England, you should go to their house. You've probably seen the portrait, the one with the boy—he made the portrait, and he's the one who's whited out of the portrait.

Oh, oh, oh! Branwell.

Yes, Branwell, right!

I'll tell you, the book I have most enjoyed—at least, if you said, "Quick, what's the book you've most enjoyed?": *Catcher in the Rye*. Again, I started the first sentence, and I was crying. I just thought, "Oh man, oh man, oh man." I just think about that. "Old Phoebe, he said Old Phoebe!" I don't get that from reading. I don't get it from prose.

Have you read it since you were young?

No, and I don't intend to. [*Laughs*]

I think that's smart.

My point is I *can* get caught by prose, but I have resistance. It's an unusual book because it can talk to you in a way that almost no—Well, you see what it is, it's theater. Because it's a character, and it's related to plays. I read plays all throughout my teens. Didn't read any novels, but—

I meant to ask you—you may have slightly known my uncle. He was roughly your age, and he was a playwright in the Phoenix Theatre group. His name was Jerome Max.

Yes, indeed, I certainly do. And I saw—oh, my memory . . .

No, it's been a long time.

I saw something of his, and/or read it. But he wrote something odd.

He wrote a number of odd things.

Name me some!

The first thing he wrote was a play called *The Exhaustion of Our Son's Love*, which was very well reviewed. It opened at some theater downtown. The week of the newspaper strike! And this is my uncle's story for years—but I admired him. That was, in a funny way, the acme of his career. But he told one story—not about you, but about your mother, from years ago.

Whoa!

No, not that kind of story! I don't know the context of this. He said that your mother at one point was in the box office at one of your productions. This must be *very* early—

It's unlikely.

Unlikely? Impossible?

Pretty impossible. She wouldn't go to the box office. But go ahead.

She wouldn't have worked in the box office?

Oh no, no . . . that would be low-class for her. She'd think, "Those are the grubby workers."

I don't think she did it to fill the job, I thought it was kind of also to connect with you—

Yeah, but that's my point. She wouldn't play in the box office. She would have played with either the patrons or a celebrity . . . As George Furth would say, "It doesn't compute."

You know, he was a playwright; he made things up.

[I back down, though I am pretty sure of the anecdote if not of the context. Besides, his mother's character is not something Sondheim is open to negotiating on.]

Anyway, I'm trying to think of the names of his plays. If you had some connection to the Phoenix crowd—he got very experimental, I think, in interesting and courageous ways.

That's where I know him from: experimental theater.

Yeah. But I don't think anyone ever really—

See, I read reviews like crazy.

Anyway, I only brought it up because there was that one story that doesn't compute.

No, doesn't compute at all. Not my mother! She *never* hung around the theater. It was completely—

Well, he died, so I can't ask him.

There's no possible way. If he ran into her, I don't know, at Sardi's, that would be a different thing.

No, no—it was his way of showing me how even in the theater when you were a success, you still needed your family, basically. That was the point of the story, maybe. I don't know.

Really naive.

Maybe it was *his* mother.

[Sondheim laughing seems the right note to leave on, and I tell him it's time for me to go.]

I left happy. Sondheim had promised me in an email an hour for the initial "confrontation" but that we could "stretch it further if we feel like it," and we had. In fact, I had been the one who ended the chat, wanting to leave a little water in the well.

The whole time we talked Sondheim had been game, interesting and interested, although I certainly hadn't asked him anything remotely intimate. In fact, I still didn't really know what that would be. The comment about his mother was certainly meaningful but the speed with which he'd offered it made me feel he was looking for a laugh. Still, I was glad that he hadn't seemed to need to present himself as perfect, so august as to be cartoony, or done with interviews, which had been my big worry. He was, in fact, pretty welcoming with me and willing to convey how he saw the world as if he had never been asked to before. In short, he had been good company. I had come expecting to start the profile we'd agreed to, while he seemed to think we were there to discuss what kind of profile we might do—a stance that gave our conversation an undertone of another audition—but that complexity didn't worry me too much. What was most important was that we had gotten along. People who get along tend to work out their differences. At the beginning, Sondheim and I had also talked about a dog to take the place of the late Max the beagle. Bernadette Peters was associated with a rescue center in Brooklyn called BARC, he told me. I would find a lovable puppy there, adding, "although what puppy isn't lovable?" He would call her.

He proved good to his word and after he hooked me up

with BARC, I called the shelter. They offered me the pick of the adoptive litter. Nothing seemed quite right to my daughter, though, and we found a puppy through a different rescue organization. Nemo arrived at our house on April Fools' Day 2017—low, long, and beige. I sent Sondheim a picture of him, and he was happy for us. "What a joy," he responded simply. No sense I had wasted his generosity or time, as I feared.

But it appeared that I already had reached the limits of his tolerance for letting me be a fly on the wall of his life. I found out almost immediately after the first interview that I could not sit in on the work around the Buñuel musical. To ask to be a witness to a meeting among people working on a show requires their trust that you aren't there to savage them, and only three days after I had left his townhouse humming "Tonight," Sondheim wrote me and said that, though he personally was fine with it, his collaborators were not, on the reasonable grounds that if I were in the room, they'd all feel self-conscious. I'd kill off, they feared, he said, the liberty to "offer stupid suggestions, take ridiculous chances and make embarrassing mistakes." Sondheim added he saw their point. He said he realized I'd be disappointed and apologized.

I had no idea why he had even felt he needed to ask his collaborators, since these were also reasonable worries for someone who had been through the critical wringer the way he had. He might even have made up his mind while still sitting in his living room with his glass of wine after saying goodbye, the seductive vapors of our chat dissipating as I went up the stairs and into the street.

I wrote him back a few days later suggesting that maybe he was overestimating how intrusive my presence would be. "It's not as if I go and sit with you and your collaborators night and day as you fumble your way toward perfection," I assured him. "It's more arthroscopic surgery than conventional." I saw now for the first time the part of him that knew how to shut the door. "I understood you completely. I never thought you meant to embarrass us," he wrote. It turned out there was another part of this late-life creative effort I had not taken into account. Sondheim said he was in a "slough of creative despond" about the work, so "the spotlight, of which I'm not too fond anyway, is even more unwelcome." This was the first news I had that the Buñuel adaptation was not proving easy for him.

There were Sondheim revivals all over New York during the following months, and I took the chance to see Sondheim off-Broadway and on-. I followed his suggestion and went to *Sweeney Todd* with my teenage son and ate real meat pies (though no eel), saw a pocket-sized *Pacific Overtures* at the Classic Stage, and took my daughter to *Sunday in the Park with George* with Jake Gyllenhaal at the Hudson Theatre. I also read the two books Sondheim had given me on his show-biz life: *Finishing the Hat* and *Look, I Made a Hat*. They were really books to browse—full of sidebars, boxed text, and lyrics with commentary—which made sense, given how Sondheim himself processed information. They had lots of good stories from inside the room—how, as he gained independence from Leonard Bernstein's lush music for *West Side*

Story, he moved his lyrics toward "the kind of imagery" he felt more connected to, "baseball, for example, rather than the night sky over Manhattan." An even more interesting story was how, with *Follies*, he rid himself of the orthodoxy that a show had to have a plot. He was at the first-anniversary party for *Fiddler on the Roof*, watching the crowd get rowdier and drunker. Eventually, a partygoer looked at his half-eaten sandwich with dismay and dropped it into the orchestra pit. "There's our show," Sondheim told his collaborator. These were just the sort of revealing, well-honed anecdotes about craft that he was denying me regarding his new musical, which felt unfair. Overall, the information in his two books was helpful—he covered every lyric he had written, including college efforts and birthday greetings for friends—but the tone was brassy: his memories were conveyed in competitive prose. Often the point of the story was that Sondheim was right, though not inevitably. He enjoyed recounting a spectacular error, too. But *someone* was right. I found the approach unsubtle, paradoxically the opposite of his lyrics.

Sondheim made a point of pointing out that the books weren't personal—"'personal' being," he asserted in the introduction to *Look I Made a Hat*, "the euphemism for 'intimate,' which is the euphemism for 'sexual.'" But that seemed to miss the point in fact. The books were impersonal because that was his first instinct in presenting himself. I thought of the 1972 book by Paul Bowles, a writer Sondheim was interested in, whose memoir *Without Stopping* William Burroughs once supposedly commented would better be titled *Without Telling*.

I wasn't blaming Sondheim, obviously. I mean, who wants to be known, really? To some extent the more incisive the questions the less one wants to spend time with the questioner—I could see that becoming an issue. I did wonder if there was anyone Sondheim actually trusted to know him intimately. Was he happy with who he was? Did he feel lonely? Who was he at three o'clock in the morning, to paraphrase Fitzgerald, a writer whose cadences I was guessing Sondheim would admire, too. (The last page of *The Great Gatsby* almost reads like a song lyric.) I was hoping over time I would know more.

OPENING
NIGHT

APRIL 2017

"I can't wait to interrupt you!"

When he shut the door on the idea of a piece on the making of the Buñuel musical, Sondheim wrote that he had hoped our paths would cross again. About two months later, they did. PEN America, the authors' rights organization, asked me if I would like to cover their spring gala, where they were going to honor Sondheim with an award for literary service. Meryl Streep would present it. Was I interested?

I was. I wanted to see Sondheim again, even if there was no immediate avenue for the profile. A public venue is often not a bad place for private confidences, and besides, I was already sensing it would not be easy to get Sondheim out of his home. He seemed well nested. It would also be interesting to learn how he handled his celebrity in and of itself. His lack of acknowledgment of his importance at our first meeting had amazed me but that had been between two people in a private place. It had been easy for us to avoid the sometimes mawkish tin-eared assaults artists we think we all have a relationship to must suffer. But how during this cere-monial evening would he fare, given the no-doubt incessant adulation those around him would shower on him?

In addition, my editors and I agreed that if the piece were smart and sharp, Sondheim might remember that I was a writer worth taking a risk for and get the profile going again. We decided I should do a piece for the Talk of the Town sec-tion of the magazine, where short articles that cover recent events like openings and visits from out-of-town celebrities go. Sondheim supported the idea.

A few weeks later, in late April, I went to pick Sondheim up at a recording studio in the neighborhood once called Hell's Kitchen and now known as Midtown West, where he was working with the cast of *Sunday in the Park*, the show starring Jake Gyllenhaal that I had just seen with my daughter. By the time I got there, the cast seemed done for the day. Crowds of singers and tech people were flowing back and forth through a warren of small rooms. I did not see Gyllenhaal or his costar Annaleigh Ashford, assuming I would recognize them. When I found Sondheim, he gave me a civil hello, as if we had had dinner a few nights be-fore, went into a bathroom, and changed into a baggy dark suit with a narrow black tie. His partner, Jeff Romley, was there, too. I took refuge in the kitchen, where there was coffee and a vending machine. I had forgotten how excluding the energy show people give off when they are together is. Soon Sondheim reappeared and we went downstairs, where a black call car was waiting to drive us to the American Museum of Natural History, up rainy Tenth Avenue, the street as stygian as it had been in the era of *West Side Story*.

We picked up our conversation where it had left off, talking about weather and dogs. He had already hinted in an earlier email that things were going better on the musical, and I was thrilled he had extracted himself from the slough. I asked him what had changed, and he mentioned that it always helped that people were bugging him for the new songs. Because of the rain we pulled up at the 77th Street entrance to the museum, under one of the rough-hewn stone staircases. We were there a little early, so there was time to kill. Sondheim seemed on edge, in his black suit with somber tie, which surprised me—I figured his life contained countless such moments. But he said that writing a speech was a novel experience for him. What people mostly wanted from him was his songs.

I mentioned that I had been to the PEN event other years, and he picked up on this.

S.S.: Oh, you've been?

I've been, yeah, 'cause I've been a literary host.

S.S.: Good grief! What's that mean? You have to be the host of the table?

No, you just have to be winsome. You're the person that they're there to be with.

S.S.: Well, it's fine, if you want to go—that's nice. You get a free trip.

But this year, they're like, "You've got to do a Talk piece."

S.S.: Why do you want to do that?

I just like PEN.

S.S.: OK, that's fair enough. As a lady friend of mine said, it's easy. Just do five minutes to the left and five minutes to the right.

[*I laugh, though it takes me a moment to get what the burlesque-hall "it" in the joke is.*] I do like these things. But I didn't realize you had a whole day before you were starting on this.

S.S.: And I'm up at seven o'clock tomorrow morning, and a whole other day.

To do more recording at the studio?

S.S.: Yep.

How did it go today?

S.S.: It went fine. It's just, like, hurry up and wait. But if you have a bouncy producer who hears it and knows how to keep things going efficiently, that helps. The real problem with these albums is, unlike pop albums, you have a *very* limited amount of time. They used to be one day or maybe two days of recording, depending on how many songs there are, and they determined that this one was worth two days' worth of recording. But if you go over time, it's a huge amount of money, and unlike pop albums, there's a *very* limited budget, so there's a tension that exists all day long . . . And when you listen to the tape later, you're saying, "Wait, isn't there *any* tape we have where she sang that note on pitch?"

So, seven tomorrow, huh?

S.S.: Well, I have to go to a doctor in order to be at the recording session, which is at nine or ten or eleven tomorrow—I forget which.

Who asked you to be the guest of honor at this?

S.S.: PEN! I mean, it was—

I didn't know if it was a personal friend, or just—

S.S.: Oh no, I don't know anybody at PEN. As a citizen, I've contributed to PEN.

[Pressing on the good news] So, you've been happily working away since I last saw you. On the new show?

S.S.: Yeah, we had a reading of it two weeks ago. And now we're working further—we'll have another reading if we can do it.

Wow! If I remember right, you had to write the second act.

S.S.: Well, I still haven't written the second act, but we have *shaped* the second act, so it's an actual second act now. The first draft of the libretto is written for the second act. And the songs are routined, so to speak, so we know where they're going to be and what they're going to be about. But I've *just* begun to write them. Whereas the first act is pretty well written now.

You put me to shame!

  S.S.: What are you talking about?!

You've been writing away as I was sitting around looking at the ceiling.

  S.S.: But how long have I been blocked? How long have I been working, you know?

I dunno, how long *have* you been working?

  S.S.: Well, we started it two years ago.

I mean, it doesn't sound that long to me, but maybe it's long for you. "How Long Have I Been Blocked?" sounds like a song. [*Sondheim laughs*.] Well, congratulations. Just to move forward is terrific. As I think you know, when you do something that nobody is particularly waiting for you to do, it's a little more complicated.

  S.S.: I know. Well, it depends on your own energy. I have to work with collaborators who expect me to have the work put together. That's not *always* true. There are a couple of shows I just went ahead and wrote on my own.

Which ones are those?

  S.S.: *Sweeney Todd* I did all by myself.

I took my son to see it. I think I wrote to you. We got the meat pies . . .

  S.S.: Kids ordinarily have a good time at that.

He had a great time.

  S.S.: It's a real kid's show.

And the staging was so good for him.

s.s.: Sure. What fun for kids!

I mean, the set, and they were so close. But I actually saw the original performance—I have no idea what I was doing. I wasn't the kind of kid who went to Broadway shows in the first weeks. But I remember I went, and I sat right behind Dick Van Dyke.

s.s.: Oh, so you couldn't see anything!

[I took from this that Dick Van Dyke is exceptionally tall, something I'd forgotten.]

All I remember is thinking how big the show seemed, and then you go to see this one and how intimate it was.

s.s.: I always meant it to be intimate, and Hal [Prince] said he just wasn't interested in doing that kind of thing. He wanted to do something epic. Hal had just had a production of *Candide* at a Broadway theater, and I wanted the Shuberts to keep the whole configuration and cover all the seats with black, and have streetlamps all around the audience, and have the beggar woman suddenly pop up next to your chair and beg for alms and things like that, so that would be fully immersed—and these are the days before immersion became popular. I just wanted to scare people. [*Laughs.*]

I noticed in this production that the boyfriend—the one who's marrying Johanna—goes around the corner, and he never comes back. You don't ever see him again.

s.s.: Oh, you know what it is? In the original, he did come back after Sweeney gets killed. After Sweeney gets killed, and Tobias goes crazy, the doors burst open and in comes

Anthony and Johanna. But because of this small cast, they chose not to—

That's so funny. So he was—

S.S.: He came back with her—she ran away, and then they came back together.

But in this production—

S.S.: In this production, no, you're absolutely right—they couldn't afford a police officer! [*Laughs.*] But it doesn't matter a lot.

No, of course, it doesn't matter at all. I don't even know why I noticed.

S.S.: Well, you're a writer! You look at plot. I understand. I do that *all* the time: "She says she has to go to the bathroom? She went to the bathroom in the first act!"

[*We get out of the car, go through an empty entrance past security guards, and begin to walk through arched hallways, hoping to be intercepted by someone official who knows where we should go.*]

I don't walk very well.

S.S.: You have a bad leg?

Yeah, I wear braces on my legs.

S.S.: Really! Where's that from?

It's neurological.

S.S.: Mine's strictly posture.

Posture?

S.S.: Posture and balance.

It's not a neurological thing?

S.S.: No. Bad posture. I spent my entire life either as the letter C or the letter L. C over the piano keys, L on the couch.

[He mimes the position of a pianist leaning over a keyboard and a writer lying on his back on a couch.

Our green room is the Theodore Roosevelt Memorial Hall. We stop and look at the diorama of Peter Stuyvesant receiving a delegation of Lenape, which one or both of us wrongly think is Peter Minuit buying Manhattan. In the background are Native American women clad only in grass skirts carrying burdens of baskets.]

I learned a lot of my anatomy here when I was a little boy.

S.S.: If you get rid of the Indians, it looks like Barbra Streisand's compound.

[We laugh at our exchange. Sondheim is humming a tune to himself which I don't recognize. I ask him what it is.]

S.S.: The end of the verse is, "Poor Peter Minuit, we can't continue it." That's the line where they say [he bought Manhattan] "for twenty-four dollars and a bottle of booze."

Who wrote it?

S.S.: Rodgers and Hart.

[I mention that I just finished writing the lyrics for a Purim play that parodies the music of Hamilton. It turns out he knows the Lin-Manuel Miranda musical well and admires it, so I plunge forward.]

You know in the song "Helpless"? I managed to rhyme "Ashi Ashi Ashi Ashareus" with "I don't know how to say this."

S.S.: [*Pauses.*] Not great . . . Are you aware of *Spamilton* and all that?

No.

S.S.: Oh, well, the guy who did *Forbidden Broadway* has done a show called *Spamilton*, which is up on 72nd Street, West 72nd Street, and it's exactly what you're talking about.

Alright, you'll appreciate this. In the parody, I also rhymed vodka with babka.

S.S.: [*Less pleased*] It doesn't rhyme.

I know it doesn't. You're so harsh!

S.S.: It's a *near*-rhyme. That's my point. If you want to do near-rhymes, don't boast about it. Don't say "I'm good at rhymes" and then do near-rhymes.

Well, what about, say, "Tyger, tyger, burning bright, / In the forests of the night, / What immortal hand or eye, / Could frame thy fearful symmetry?"

S.S.: What made you think it was pronounced "symme-tri"?

I don't know. [*And I don't. I just always assumed it was recited that way.*]

S.S.: Alright, well, for centuries, and right up until 1940, these two words rhymed in songs, poems, everything: "rain" and "again."

But only in England, right?

s.s.: No! Here too!

In ordinary speech?

s.s.: Oh no, no, no. In songs and visual works.

What's the best rhyme you've ever heard?

There isn't one. OK, I'll tell you another one. Yip Harburg rhymed "everybody" with "la-di-da-di."

Who did that?

s.s.: Yip Harburg.

I don't know him.

s.s.: [*He's happy to enlighten me about something he loves.*] He was one of the great lyric writers. *Finian's Rainbow. Wizard of Oz.* He's responsible for "Somewhere Over the Rainbow." That's my favorite. I'll tell you what it is: It's not about the rhymes, because that's not hard to do. It's, How does the rhyme work with the sense of the song? Let's say, "Rhyme orange." It's easy to rhyme orange. It's easy to use a part-rhyme. Porringer. "I have an orange or a porringer." But it's about making a rhyme that clicks. It's like sinking a pool ball into the pocket. The rhyme goes, *Oop!* And does that to the thought and makes the thought delightful in some way. So, it's the usefulness of a clever rhyme.

Alright, so what's the best rhyme you . . .

S.S.: I don't know. I have to think. I'll tell you, when I preen, it's when I see a show of my own and think, "Yeah! That really works!"

[Meryl Streep arrives, wearing a black jacket and black-and-white-striped pants.]

S.S.: Hi there!

MERYL STREEP: Hiiii there!

S.S.: It's so sweet of you to do this, and generous. This is D. T. Max! I know him as D.T. You look great!

M.S.: Thank you! It's my springtime outfit.

S.S.: It's your harlequin outfit. [*Streep laughs.*] It looks great. Are you connected with PEN in some way?

M.S.: No, no.

S.S.: They just asked you to do this? I mean, they roped you in?

M.S.: No, it's because I love you.

[This causes Sondheim to miss a beat.]

S.S.: You should know that D.T. is writing a piece on this for Talk of the Town, so don't say anything, Meryl—just be careful.

[We begin to walk again, now three of us, through endless confusing passageways. Echoes of The Discreet Charm of the Bourgeoisie. *As if in the movie, the sound of people having fun gets louder and louder but remains just out of reach.*

We are stopped by some PEN staff members who ask Sondheim and Streep to hold signs to free Oleg Sentsov, the Ukrainian filmmaker sentenced by the Russians after the invasion of the Crimea, and take their picture. They agree. PEN asks them to publicize the cause on social media, but neither has any. (The international campaign on Sentsov's behalf was successful. He was released in a prisoner swap two years later.)

As we trudge along, I again bring up the subject of "babka" and "vodka" with Sondheim. I'm violating my own rule not to compete with him, but I love the rhyme—or near-rhyme—and I'd like some acknowledgment, at least of the form, which I enjoy more than pure rhyme.]

S.S.: What happens—when did the B become a D? Come on! You know they don't rhyme.

Yeah, but I thought that was part of the point. It's not a pure rhyme—
S.S.: If you think part of the fun is singing off-pitch, then that's your taste, but that's my idea of not-fun, because it's always a disappointment. If you're aware of my thought and you think—

Well, what would you think, for the purpose of the Jewish prayer—
S.S.: Well, you're talking to somebody—I didn't grow up Reform or anything. I didn't go to a temple until I was twenty-two. I know nothing whatsoever. What I can tell you is . . . I

haven't been to Passover since Lenny [Bernstein]. And that was a pretty long time ago.

[We continue marching through the gloaming. I tell Sondheim a Jewish joke. (I forget which, but likely learned from my father-in-law, who has dozens.) Sondheim responds that he knows only "the kreplach joke." I ask him to tell it to me.]

S.S.: A little kid says to his mother, "I hate kreplach." His mother says, "It's tomatoes and onions and everything you love. Taste it!" The son does and says, "It's still kreplach." [*He pauses.*] That's a profound joke.

[At last we make it to the balcony above the main hall; hundreds of tables are below us, and the vast blue whale hangs above our heads.]

S.S.: Whale, here we are! [*Streep and I laugh.*]

[Waiters appear, and we are offered wine.]

S.S.: D.T., I've discovered that you look like Geoffrey Rush, but I'm sure we've been over that before . . . The fact that you wear glasses makes you look Rush-like. He did *Forum* down in Australia, and I got to know him.

[I tell him I'm more often mistaken for the Nicolas Cage—or was when we were both younger—but he sees Rush. I settle them for an interview at an out-of-the-way table.]

So, the slightly awkward thing is that actually what I'd like to do for the Talk piece is hear you guys talk . . . I'm gonna ask, just because I just watched *Into the Woods* last night, which I loved. I know I sound like a reporter, but how did you meet? Through *Into the Woods*?

S.S.: Noooo!

M.S.: Long before that!

Tell me how you met.

S.S.: Let her do it, then I'll correct it.

M.S.: I didn't have to bring my husband, because there you are!

S.S.: Now you have a portrait of Meryl's marriage: it's called the Bickersons.

M.S.: I was in a production of *The Frogs*, which was at Yale when I was a first-year student. And I was in the chorus. And he was very legendary.

S.S.: It was 1973. It took place in the Yale swimming pool.

And you spotted her on the chorus?

M.S.: No, no, I don't think he even noticed me. But it was really hilarious. There was a lot of vying to get into the chorus from the women in the drama school because most of the cast were young men in bathing suits. Everybody wanted to be in the chorus! [*Laughs*]

S.S.: The Yale swimming team played the frogs.

M.S.: And they were fantastic.

S.S.: This was a notion of Burt Shevelove's, who had to have done it prewar, when he was head of the Dramat there. Burt had directed it back then. And then the war came along, and Burt became a director and producer, and then Robert Brustein, who was at Yale, said to Burt, "I would love to do *The Frogs* again." And the original one had been written by students. And Burt said, "Would you write some songs for this one, Steve?" Ordinarily, I would say no, because Brustein hated my work, and did everything he could to destroy my career, such as it was. *Really*, really hated my stuff, and said awful things about me, and—

M.S.: **He loved me! [*Laughs*]**

S.S.: [*Laughs*] Well, it occurred to me to be blond! But so, I said yes, because Burt had just done me a huge favor. He had put together a charity thing of mine that was done at the Shubert Theatre that had been started by incompetents. And Burt, who lived in England, came all the way over to the United States to save my ass and make this into a very good charity event. So I owed him a favor, so I did *The Frogs*. But no, I didn't get to know any of the chorus, because we had only ten days to write songs.

That's amazing!

M.S.: **Ten days. That's all *you* need! [*Laughs*]**

S.S.: Well, I only wrote four, but they were long! And so then, it was staged in the swimming pool. And Larry Blyden played Dionysus—

[While we talk, other people are gathering for the party, milling, uniting, and chatting. The band has assembled and is warming up loudly.]

Why are they playing "Sunrise, Sunset"? Do they think you wrote it?

S.S.: Now, this you're not allowed to say! See, I wrote the score of *Fiddler*. Sheldon [Harnick] and Jerry [Block] were Communists, and so I had to . . . [*He pauses, goes from cut-up to authority.*] They're playing hits.

So, anyway, we didn't actually meet. I actually thought you were going to say someplace else.

But you already knew who he was?

M.S.: Oh yeah, 'cause he was a god.

S.S.: No, not really. I had only written a few shows by then. This is the year—

M.S.: [*Sarcastically*] Yeah, only *Gypsy*.

S.S.: Yeah. *West Side Story*, *Gypsy*, and *Forum*. And then *Anyone Can Whistle*, which, I have to say, they stripped my epaulets after that. [*Laughs*] But where we *really* met was, we had a mutual friend, Liam Neeson and his wife, Natasha.

M.S.: Oh my God, do I miss her!

S.S.: And they liked to give holiday parties, which featured charades, which Meryl happens to like a lot. [*Streep laughs.*] And so I met her, really, up there, at a charades game. Mia Farrow was a great friend of Natasha's, and said, "You want to come along? Take me to this party?" And I said, "Sure."

M.S.: **You had no idea of the cutthroat world we were entering.**

S.S.: Well, the trouble was that half of the people were not interested in the games, and the other half were. And it's very difficult to play games when half the people are feeling like fools. [*Streep laughs.*] I remember one of the guests was Ismail Merchant. And a few people thought, "Oh, well, he's Indian. He doesn't understand the language." But no, it wasn't that. He just didn't like to play games! A lot of people don't like to do that! People like Meryl and me, we *love* that kind of game. We enjoy making fools of ourselves trying to act out, you know, "Areopagitica" or something like that. That's the fun. I play a different kind of charades than she does. I play running charades, in which there are two teams that are in relay. She likes to play the kind where her team makes up all the things, and then our team acts them out, and they giggle at what assholes we are as we're doing them.

M.S.: [*Laughs delightedly.*]

S.S.: It's true! And I tried to inculcate them into running charades, in which one person, before the party, makes a list of charades, and then each team chooses a captain—they go together. And they each go back to their teams and act out whatever the first on the list is. Whichever team gets it first, the player that guessed it on that team runs to the person who had made the list—

You give your charade to the other people?

S.S.: Right, yeah.

M.S.: It was too complicated to do when you're drunk, as we were! You couldn't possibly do it. [*To Sondheim*] Did you ever play that one at Natasha's, which is my favorite game—we still play, and we call it "Natasha's game"—which is that you go through the house and you get a bunch of books, and you have two teams, and you open the book. One person is the reader, and they open the book, and they tell you the title, the author, and then you write down what you think is the first line in the book. It is the most wonderful game!

[*To Sondheim*] **You'd be good at that.**

M.S.: Oh my God, we used to play this endlessly—

S.S.: I can't *wait* to interrupt you.

M.S.: I noticed that!

S.S.: This game was *invented* by—

M.S.: By you?

S.S.: By *me* and Mary Ann Madden.

M.S.: [*With feigned anger*] Goddamn it!

S.S.: There used to be a game called Dictionary. And one evening, Mary Ann said, "Why use a dictionary? Why don't we do it out of *Bartlett's Quotations*?" So, you know the way Dictionary works—*Bartlett's* is another version of it, where you take *Bartlett's*, and one person reads an author, and then you write down the quote from that author.

M.S.: **That's good. It's harder—**

S.S.: No, I'll tell you what makes it better than you think. Almost ninety percent of the authors in *Bartlett's* are people you have never heard of. "Ella Mae Sargent, 1853 to 1886." "Lord Something"—so you can make up anything. You don't have to be well read, which I'm not.

M.S.: **Yeah, but it has to sound like something. Here's the thing about if you make it a book: we have had many games in our house where the eight-year-old wins, because the first line is, "The sun never came up that day." You know, in other words, everybody writes down their idea of what the first line of the book is, and then the reader reads them all out, including the right one—the actual one—and people vote on which is the authentic first line of the book.**

S.S.: The thing is, in our game the eight-year-olds *also* win. The very first one I played up at Leonard Bernstein's house, Jamie, who was eleven years old, won. That's over Lenny and Felicia and me all these elegant people, and we're all figuring out, "I see, it's a nineteenth-century writer, and she would have written with . . ."

[The band strikes up another tune. It's one of Sondheim's!]

Sweeney Todd? Finally, they got the right composer in the right room with the right music. It took them a while.

[Sondheim laughs lightly. This is something he takes for granted.]

Do you guys see each other a lot or never?

S.S.: Never.

M.S.: No. Well, we had dinner last summer.

S.S.: Yeah. Very occasionally.

M.S.: Because you're working all the time.

S.S.: That's one thing. But we plan.

M.S.: We plan, and then he cancels, and then we plan, and then he cancels!

S.S.: Well, there's a third person, which is Christine Baranski, as part of this group. And she does a lot of canceling.

M.S.: Yeah. And, you know, we're trying to get everybody together.

S.S.: It's too bad, because we do live in vaguely the same neighborhood, in Connecticut.

M.S.: He and Christine live ten minutes from each other, and I have to drive an hour.

And when you made *Into the Woods*, you probably didn't see a lot of each other either, right? Because you weren't on the set.

S.S.: We did at the beginning, because I wrote a song for her.

Yeah, I was going to ask you about that. I listened to it last night—the bonus track. [*The song is called "She'll Be Back."*]

S.S.: I love it.

Were you sad that it didn't wind up in the movie?

M.S.: I was, but I really understood why, thematically.

S.S.: Me too.

M.S.: It made great sense.

S.S.: I think, in fact, when I wrote it, I said, "You're going to cut this song, because it is going to hold up the action. And it's wonderful to have her sing a solo, but . . ." And sure enough, they cut it.

You sing it so beautifully.

S.S.: Yeah. But you can always tell when you're writing something—whether it's good or bad. I learned that from Oscar Hammerstein, who was completely ruthless about cutting songs. When they wrote *Oklahoma!* their big song was a song called "Boys and Girls Like You and Me," which was played in the overture, sung in the first act, played in the entr'acte, and reprised in the second act. [*He pauses for effect.*] And they cut it in New Haven.

M.S.: Wow! Let's get a hold of it!

S.S.: Well, it eventually ended up in an MGM movie, and Judy Garland sang it, and then it was cut.

But you autographed Meryl's sheet music for that song, right? With the inscription "Don't fuck it up"? I read this—

S.S.: How did you find that?

It's online.

S.S.: She must have told somebody. I didn't tell anybody.

It popped right up!

S.S.: He spends his life looking at chat rooms and YouTube . . . but no, he's really a literary person. [*I'm being teased.*]

I use it to figure out where my kids are. [*Streep and Sondheim laugh*.] So, you guys have no current plans to collaborate on anything at the moment?

S.S.: No, I wish we did.

M.S.: I've written a new thing, Steve. [*Laughs*]

S.S.: Well, in actuality—we actually discussed something in London. But I'm not gonna tell you what it is.

M.S.: I'm hoping. I'm sitting on my hands and hoping.

S.S.: I'm thinking. I have actually given some thought to it.

A full-length theatrical work with music?

S.S.: I haven't—that's as far as we go.

[*To Streep*] And you know what this thing is?

M.S.: No!

S.S.: No. Well, we decided on something that interested us mutually.

That's exciting. Is it bigger than a bread box?

S.S.: Don't probe, because we've done nothing but talk about it. It hasn't gotten any farther than that. But we have, and I have not forgotten.

M.S.: And you know, the kiss of death for a new project is to talk about it before it's become a thing. It's a *kinahora*. [*She taps the table.*] You don't buy a crib—

S.S.: Yeah. And you don't tell everybody "I'm pregnant!" You don't do that.

People do that now.

M.S.: They post their sonograms!

S.S.: Oh my God!

They do. Is that inviting the evil hand?

S.S.: Yeah, I think it is. I think it's inviting the curse.

But medical care is so much better than it was.

S.S.: I'll tell you one thing: When you say, "Guess what? I had the baby yesterday," the listener is *so* bored. You know, you've been waiting for the premiere? Enough already!

[*To Sondheim*] You're an only child, aren't you? You were it? You were the blessing—

S.S.: Blessing? No. My mother didn't want me, and my father—

[Just at this moment of potential intimacy, a waiter urges us to get to our table. We shuffle to our seats. We are right near the stage, seated

with four or five other people who don't seem to know Streep and Sondheim well. There are maybe a hundred tables around us, and over our heads the enormous blue whale disports. Most people affect not to notice Streep—or they are too busy weaving their own webs— and they well may not recognize Sondheim. I apologetically ask to swap seats with Romley so I can sit next to his partner, explaining that I need to continue reporting.

The program begins. The then-president of PEN, Andrew Solomon, talks about writers in peril, his amplified voice echoing in the vast hall. Streep is second in the program. She introduces Sondheim and tells the story of The Frogs. Then Sondheim comes up and speaks. He looks nervous and small at the podium.

After his brief remarks, in which he talks about supporting a program for young playwrights and ends by saying, "I'm also glad you like my songs," he comes back down to applause. It strikes me how careful his speech was, how well crafted to make people appreciate without resenting him. Now Audra McDonald performs "The Glamorous Life," Sondheim's piercing take on celebrity parents. She breaks off in the middle and starts again. Sondheim watches affably from his seat. You have to suppose this is an ordinary occurrence for him—to hear his own music as if it's the wind in the air. There is great applause when McDonald finishes.]

S.S.: [*Appreciatively*] You either have the vocal cords or you don't! [*To Streep, teasing me again.*] He's reviewing it. He didn't like the rhyme in the third chorus. [*Laughter*]

How often did she rehearse that, you think?

S.S.: She's sung it many times. That's a favorite song of hers. It's from the movie of *Night Music*. There's a song called "Glamorous Life" in the stage show, which is not this song.

I see—I didn't know the song.

S.S.: Nobody does. It's sung by the little girl. And I wrote it for the movie. I don't know why she picked up on it, but she sings that often at gatherings like this. You'd have to ask her about it. My guess is it relates to her life.

I didn't get the joke when she started again. Is that written into the song?

S.S.: No, no—she skipped a whole section.

Oh, she did? I thought she was joking.

S.S.: No, just, you know, stage fright. But you know she's sung it many times . . . nobody sings that song except her. I happen to love the song, so I'm glad she does it.

[A guest comes up and discusses meeting Sondheim at a White House State Dinner. This reminds me I too once saw Sondheim in Washington . . .]

I saw you years ago, with Frank Rich, actually, in DC, at the Kennedy Center. I don't remember why you were there.

S.S.: We did talks all over the country. That was a gig we did at least a dozen times. In every major city, from Seattle to Atlanta.

All I remember about it is that you talked about why you hadn't produced *Assassins* at the time. And I was amazed that you could take a piece of work that good and say, "Well, the time's not right." I thought, "Whoa! If I had a piece of work that good, you wouldn't keep me from putting that thing on."

S.S.: Yes, you would, if you thought it was gonna cause—

What year was it? I forget. What had just happened?

S.S.: Obama had just got elected, I think.

No, no, it's earlier. It has to be before the second Bush.

S.S.: Well, anyway, the point was, it was a dangerous thing to say. I mean, we're doing it again this summer, at City Center, and there's a good deal of worry—

Really?

S.S.: Sure. Right-wingers will say it advocates assassination.

I remember you said something had happened—when was it written?

S.S.: Well, the first thing that happened was the Gulf War was on, so it got postponed.

Oh, you wrote it that late!

S.S.: 1990. And then when the revival was supposed to happen, something just as bad—I don't remember. Anyway, it's incendiary, you know.

I don't remember it that way. I remember it as humanizing—which I guess is incendiary on some level.

S.S.: To some people, it is.

But I mean, it's not—

S.S.: You can't just say, "Let's do it anyway." You're putting the actors' lives in danger. You're putting the theater in danger. It isn't just you jerking off. You have a number of people who are vulnerable because of what you're saying.

[I bring up now one of the things I'd been mulling since our first meeting.]

So, I know you're not a big reader, but—

S.S. I'm certainly not!

Is that cognitively, you just don't—

S.S.: I told you, I'm very slow.

Why?

S.S.: It takes me a long time to read. Simple as that. And so I don't get into the book soon enough to want to continue . . . I'm very ill read. Very slow. A fast mind and a slow reader.

But do you read poetry?

S.S.: I used to, because that's short and mysterious. And I read plays—dialogue, I always loved to read. I read a *lot* of plays as a kid. Lots. Lots!

You don't seem like a person who doesn't finish books.

S.S.: I'll tell you why: I read book reviews.

That works!

S.S.: And I told Arthur [Laurents] this, and there's the line in *Gypsy* where the mother says to Gypsy, when Gypsy is swanning around in her dressing room, and the mother is sneering at her, "You, who read book reviews like they was books!" He got that from me.

I read a lot of detective stories when I was in my teens, but I loved history. I read a lot of John Dickson Carr, Rex Stout, people like that.

M.S.: I'm so obsessed with reading right now.

And what are you reading?

M.S.: Right now—

S.S.: [*It's Streep's turn to be teased.*] *Vogue* and *Cosmopolitan* and the Style section of the *Times*.

M.S.: No, I'm reading Jane Mayer's *Dark Money*.

S.S.: Wow. Wow! I'll bet that's good.

M.S.: She's really, really good.

She's a colleague of mine—she's probably here tonight, actually.

S.S.: My guess is there are a lot of people here we'd like to meet.

M.S.: I know. And now we're stuck next to each other. [*Laughs*]

S.S.: No, and we don't know what they look like!

M.S.: [*Laughs*] It's true!

S.S.: Unlike actors . . .

[*A well-known film director approaches and introduces himself to discuss the new production of* Sunday in the Park with George.]

I saw it with my daughter . . . I thought that it really came alive in the second act. Maybe that's just the way it's written.

S.S.: I liked the whole thing. I liked it the whole way through.

When he does "Art Isn't Easy"—

S.S.: He doesn't do "Art Isn't Easy." That's the girl.

Sorry, when all the people freeze—

S.S.: It's called "Putting It Together."

[Sondheim is affable but fast. I'm trying to get my footing.]

It's a classic song of yours where the irony is all in the kind of unspoken. I thought it totally came alive there. But the first act is tricky because he doesn't sing that much, right?

S.S.: Well, he sings quite a lot in the first act. Like "Finishing the Hat." And "The Dog Song." And "Color and Light." He sings quite a lot. Maybe you just weren't impressed by it.

No, no, I love the whole show. I just felt like there was a *moment* when he sang that song. Because I had heard it, but I'd actually never seen it. I said to my daughter, "I feel like the show's over. What happens now?"

S.S.: A lot of people have criticized the show for being over in the first act. "Why'd they write the second act?" The first act is a *stunt* if it's by itself. This revival, however, many people who saw it the first time and said they didn't get the second act got it this time.

Why do you think that is?

S.S.: Because I think time has passed, and they now know what the show is. And Jake and Annaleigh have something going on between them that's worth watching. Anyway, we recorded the first part of it today. So you'll hear it again.

I want to. And if you want to meet someone here, if I know them, I'm happy to—

s.s.: No, no, I don't want to meet anybody. We were talking about the fact that I don't read, and this room is filled with famous novelists and essayists, whom I'd like to meet, except I don't want to meet them because I don't know their work. I mean, I know what they've written, but I've not read—

Maybe you want to meet your publisher.

s.s.: I've met my publisher. And my editor must be here to-night.

Did he play much of a role in shaping your books?

s.s.: He did—he said, "Why don't you do more of this and less of this?" So it wasn't editing, like, "I think this clause is klutzy." It was editing like, "Why do you go on about this show, but you don't tell us anything about that one?" Or, "Why do you go on about the show, and you don't go on about her?" That's editing.

And were you responsive?

s.s.: Of course. I'm a collaborator by nature.

And how did you write when you're not a reader? Was it the same thing?

s.s.: I'm writing plays! All through my teens, I read plays.

It's slightly different, though.

s.s.: I read dramatic structures that you put on a stage where people put on makeup and pretend to be other people. That's entirely different than writing a novel or an essay.

Right.

[A steadily increasing stream of people are coming by to introduce themselves and say how much his work means to them and it's beginning to wear on his nerves.]

S.S.: You know, somebody's got to write a book called *I Hate to Interrupt You*. Somebody's gotta write a book: *I Hate to Interrupt You, But I'm Gonna Do It Anyway!* They don't hate to interrupt you. They *love* to interrupt you! It's a complete lie— or an alternative fact. "I hate to interrupt you. But would you mind stopping your conversation and talking to *me*?!"

Do you have this happen to you all the time?
S.S.: Yes. All the time.

Do you remember when it started in your career?
S.S.: Yeah, as soon as I got known, it happened. As he said, it happens as soon as you're in *any* way relevant. *[He pauses.]* Don't make it sound like—now I'm gonna sound like I'm bitchy. Please don't make me sound bitchy.

You had success early—
S.S.: I got panned for *Forum*! One critic said, "Sondheim should not write songs."

But when Meryl says you were already legendary—
S.S.: That was 1973.

How much later was that?
S.S.: Oh, I started in '57. Sixteen years. And eight shows.

You're not going to agree with me, but I still say there's a difference between being panned and being ignored.

S.S.: No, there is! And what was great about my first review, which was on *West Side Story*, was that, in the *New York Times*, I was ignored. I was the only person who was not mentioned. And in the *Trib*, I was panned. So I knew right away that it's worse to be ignored. It's so much better to be panned.

Someone told me you don't like *West Side Story*.

S.S.: No, no, no. I didn't like my lyrics, because it feels so written. It doesn't feel spontaneous.

[A woman comes up and simply says, "Thank you, thank you so much," and then leaves.]

Doesn't that warm the cockles of your heart a little bit?

S.S.: It does in a way. She means it. She wanted to come up, and it's all genuine.

This was a huge issue for David Foster Wallace—this thing where people come up to you, and they're responding to your work, but they're misinterpreting the person who sits behind the work. They think they have a familiarity.

S.S.: No, but almost everybody thinks that an artist is his work, whether it's a writer . . . occasionally they're right, but most of the time they're not.

There's something about touching the hand—

S.S.: Exactly.

I don't think, with your work, that people think—

    S.S.: No, most people think I'm cold and cerebral. That's been my reputation.

They think you're Bobby.

    S.S.: Exactly—that's another one.

Well, if you were to throw a dart at one character you created, would there be anyone who had more aspects of yourself?

    S.S.: There's no character I care about that doesn't have some of me in him. Every writer writes in part of himself, but no there's no character—

Franklin Shepard, Inc.?

    S.S.: I'm not—that is as far away from myself as I go.

But are you the guy singing that song?

    S.S.: No, I'd have nobody to sing it to.

I love that song. When my son was three or four, I would sing that song with him. He had no clue what it was about. It's not that personal to me, but I would always tear up at the part where he talks about flying off to California. I don't even know why.

    S.S.: Did you often leave the house?

Yeah—actually—being a journalist—

    S.S.: We were just talking about a father who leaves his house to do an assignment. That's you.

[I had not thought of this before, a useful caution that if it's so hard to know yourself, how likely are you really to ever know

someone else?] So maybe that's why I teared up. But I'm a huge crier.

S.S.: Me too.

I cried at the end of *Sunday in the Park*.

S.S.: You're saying that as if it's unusual—*most* people cried.

When she wheels out in a wheelchair? My God. It just turned on the waterworks. [*To Meryl*] Do you cry at the end of *Sunday in the Park*?

M.S.: Oh, I cry all the way through because I know where we're going. That's my problem. I cry at the beginning!

S.S.: [*My turn to be teased again*] He thinks he's *unusual* for crying at the second act.

"Children and Art," man. You probably wrote it thinking, "I'll make some yutz cry in the fifth row."

S.S.: No! But the thing is, I got a number of letters, a *large* number of letters, from commuters who came to see the show who said, "On my way home on the train, I suddenly found myself crying," and I know *exactly* what it's about. It's about, "Wouldn't it be wonderful to live in that park?" What that park represents—it's a work of art. I'm talking about Seurat. I get it.

[There is activity on the stage again after the break for dinner. The presentation of awards is about to begin.

An editor approaches us, and I introduce him to Sondheim.]

EDITOR: I'm a man for whom *Sweeney Todd* has been a lifelong, deep, deep dive.

S.S.: It is for all murderers.

EDITOR: I know—the murder at the heart of love is amazing to me.

S.S.: How nice to meet you.

[The editor departs.]

S.S.: Is he a violent young man?

[Sondheim confers with Romley.]

S.S.: We're going home.

You're going to sneak out before—?

S.S.: No, because I have to get up . . . Jeff, we should go home and feed the pups. I don't know where my award is but— we'll say good night to you. If I didn't have to get up early in the morning, I would sit here and drink and meet people.

Alright, thank you for including me. Much appreciated.

S.S.: Be kind.

At PEN I had inevitably been intoxicated by ambient fame. In Sondheim's and my search for the party, we had come upon a media couple that I'd known for a long time. Upon seeing me with Sondheim, their spines snapped straight and they greeted me with mile-wide smiles, as if they'd been waiting their whole lives for a chance to see me again. I knew the pride I felt as a result was fake, but I realized at least at one point Sondheim would have felt it, too. How, I wondered, and when had he overcome it?

If he had ever enjoyed being a cynosure, by this time Sondheim clearly liked only aspects of it. He appreciated when people told him his songs were important to them, but more intimate revelations of devotion left him cold—and, in fact, seemed to bother him. Giving speeches, having people interrupt his conversation with "I once met you's," being looked at by strangers was not his thing. It violated his sense of himself as fundamentally offstage. And his rejoinders seemed to suggest to interlopers that he felt that way.

That night, I felt fortunate to fall within his inner circle. With Streep and Romley I was part of his protective barrier, not the ones who interrupt but are interrupted, and, to use a favorite word of his, I was flattered. Within that zone our conversation had flourished. Sondheim, an eye on his legacy, seemed happy to teach me what I already should have known, and the banter, though obviously competitive, was something I thought we could both sustain. I had grown up with it in that too-large West Side apartment, and I suspected that despite the antagonism he felt toward his bizarre mother, so had he. There was no doubt also a lot of it at the Hammersteins' during the famous summers he spent practically living with the family.

It was also clear to me that competitiveness was central to Sondheim's makeup—both in his career but also in his relationship with other men—at least that's how it felt to me when we were both talking to Streep. It was something I looked forward to asking him about more later, when we knew each other better. Which would possibly lead us into a discussion of what it had been like for Sondheim to be gay during the time he was becoming well known, how he felt it had shaped his relationships in high school, college, and the theater, a discussion that, as far as I knew—and I had read a fair number of interviews by now—he'd never had with any candor. Indeed, that and how he'd felt growing up Jewish seemed two areas of Sondheim's psyche where he'd by now attained almost a reflexive level of deflection. (Asked by an interviewer once if he had faced anti-Semitism in his professional life, he answered, "My God—in the theater? In musicals? Name me three gentile composers.")

I felt more confidence I understood Sondheim at least a little as I drove home to New Jersey that evening, my tuxedo jacket crumpled in the back of my car. It was one thing to present yourself in your living room and hold court for a couple of hours, but watching how Sondheim held up at his ten thousandth public event under a constant barrage of adoration made me feel I had seen him a bit more as he was, the makeup smeared as the evening hours went on. He was becoming three-dimensional to me.

NEW YORK
RUN

JULY 2017

*"Go ahead and ask away—
whatever you want."*

Talk of the Town pieces are short—no longer than a thousand words. I felt that in writing such a brief article I had a good chance of pleasing Sondheim. Profiles were the sorts of things he might admire without finishing, while Talk pieces were little puzzles, and, oh, how he loved puzzles. As I wrote, I managed to embed a few of his song titles in my sentences: children and art, old friends. I imagined his pleasure as he noticed them. I thought he'd also like how the piece sketched in so much about our evening without actually narrating it, much as a lyric might.

The very next day after the piece came out in the

New Yorker, I received the email I hoped for. Sondheim wrote me that he was charmed by the article. Lin-Manuel Miranda also apparently read it. "Sondheim. Streep. playing. charades. I . . . WANNA BE IN THE ROOOOOOOOOOWOWOOOOOM," he tweeted the next day.

I was excited but a little unsure what to do next. It took me a little more than a month to figure out how to ask: Could we see each other again? "We would not have to spend a ton of time together to get it done," I promised. "It ain't a marriage or even dating—and we can time it for the new show. But for Pete's sake, let's get a piece into the magazine that's worthy of the creator of *Sweeney Todd* and *Merrily* and *Company* and, yes, *Anyone Can Whistle*. Now I've said it," I concluded.

His response was as terse as it was gratifying: "If the magazine wants to do another and you want to write it, okay with me."

I was excited, and I also felt I knew how to go forward with him now. My Sondheim interview rules: Don't put him on a pedestal, but don't fence with him either. Ask him about his work. And if you do these things, if you ask him about his music and his lyrics and his technical creative process, he may over time become open to deeper reflections.

I did not take him up on his invitation to meet for almost another month. I knew assuming too much familiarity would be a mistake. Sondheim, despite his informality, obviously had his boundaries. His offers to get together always had time limits and were couched by the caution that he would be working before and afterward.

But it was encouraging news that he was moving forward with the show so fast—I did not want to miss any exciting moments of creativity I might be around him for.

So in mid-July I wrote him and we agreed I would come by a week later at 5:30—this would give us enough time to talk before he left to see a show afterward. Sondheim later emailed to delay a week—his music assistant, Peter Jones, could bring the dogs down to the city, so he could stay in Connecticut and work on Buñuel longer. More good news in its way.

I googled Jones's name and found that he had been Sondheim's first acknowledged significant relationship, not had until the composer-lyricist was in his sixties. That seemed improbable. I also found something oddly un-Sondheim-like he had said back in 2009 about the relationship in an interview: "Once I had tasted the joys of living with some-one, I wanted to live with someone else when it broke up." If I were playing Bartlett's and asked to identify the source of that quote, Sondheim would have been the last name I picked. But, well, who knew? One of my favorite quotes was by Kant (I first came upon it as a book title by Isaiah Berlin, the nonmusical one) to the effect that nothing straight was ever made from the crooked timber of humanity. I didn't know if Sondheim craved intimacy or not, but I was certain it was nothing he wanted or would be able to discuss with me at this point. He kept his romantic relationships in the shadows, not that I remotely blamed him for it.

We fixed on a day a week later, the twenty-sixth of July.
I offered to bring kreplach, belaboring the joke, but he said
he had everything from "cheese to Quaker Oats." The day
I was supposed to visit, though, he wrote again to tell me
he'd suffered from an episode of atrial fibrillations early that
morning. The attacks, he explained, were "fairly frequent,"
and left him with a lot of debilitating gastric reflux. I was
completely surprised. This was my first news that he had any
health issues. Up till now, he had seemed like a just-seventy-
year-old playing a nearly-ninety-year-old. I mean not just
his mind, which was obviously still state-of-the-art, but
even his movements, his hearing, the quality of focus when
he looked at you seemed barely middle-aged. He assured me
that I would likely be able to visit that afternoon anyway,
asking only that I call first to make sure he was well enough
to meet.

By the appointed hour, he had recovered, but the incident
added a new nuance to our conversation. When one person
is ill, the other naturally becomes a caregiver of some sort.
When I got to his townhouse, was spilled into the living
room, plopped onto the same seat, and graced with a glass of
rosé, he brought up his health for the first time—specifically,
a blood thinner he took for the fibrillations.

There's no antidote for it if I'm in an auto accident, but—

You mean there's no way to reverse it?
Yeah, no way to make the blood clot faster. But the point is
that it's fine. I cut my thumb.

And you bled?

Like you wouldn't believe! Out in the country, at midnight, I was all alone—this was about six months ago—and like an idiot I was cleaning out a can, and I cleaned it with a sponge, and it went right that way [*he makes a slicing gesture*], and it started bleeding, and I thought, "Oh God." And I started to wrap things around it, and I called the neighbor, and because I don't drive at night, I said, "Will you drive me to the emergency room? Because I can't stop bleeding." He came in, and it looked like a serial killer had been there. There was blood all over the ice, all over the refrigerator, on the walls, in the sink . . .

On the windows.

Exactly! Just from opening it. Because I had put ice on it—opened it, and it left blood all over the thing, and when he came in, he went [*he mimes a horrified face*] and I said, "No, no, it's just my thumb!"

I'm impressed you drive at all, as a New York boy.

Oh, I love to drive; it's just my eyes now.

I didn't pick up driving until my mid-twenties, because I had no need.

Oh no. I got my first car when I was twenty, as a graduation present, because that summer after I graduated college, I went to work as an apprentice at Westport Country Playhouse. We had a place in Stamford, Connecticut, so I had to commute—it was about a fifteen-, twenty-minute drive—and so Dad gave me a secondhand, small Chevy, and that's how I learned to drive.

[Wrestling with the incongruity of interviewing someone who just had a severe medical incident.]

So, we'll do this as long as you're comfortable. If you don't feel well, we'll pick it up later.

My energy level is a little low.

Yeah, I get that. I was just going to propose that we talk the way we're talking. I'll figure out the form later.

Go ahead and ask away—whatever you want.

Just because I haven't seen you for a month or so, how's the work on the show going?

It's very slow. The older I get, the slower I get at everything I do. That's not unusual. But the energy level, unlike some people—there are people who carry their energy. You know I'm fond of saying George Bernard Shaw kept writing plays until he was ninety-four. Of course, the last fifteen years they were *terrible*, but he did write them! And then I was stunned, although I suppose not surprised, when I went to the Guggenheim and saw its exhibition of late Picasso. There was a drawing, and it said, you know, "May 16, 1934, 4:30." Then you went to the next drawing: "May 16, 1934, 9:15." Then you went to the next one: "May 17, 7 A.M." He just could not stop. And I thought, "That's what I want to do." And it was the last couple years of his life.

[He must be misremembering the date of the anecdote for it to make sense—Picasso was just past fifty in 1934, but I don't notice.]

That's amazing. I remember you saying on our car ride that you knew where the songs had to go.

That's right. I routine things—I think most writers do—with a book writer. We say, "Where are songs helpful? Where are they possible but unnecessary?" Blah, blah, blah. I try to write songs that are necessary. It seems to be important to keep the pace going, because I think an audience senses when songs are merely reiterating what you already know, or when they're ahead of you. So I routine them, and then I try to do it chronologically, because often you want to write something, then pick up the musical theme, or even the lyrical theme, and use it later on. I like to make the collection of songs have some kind of unity—not just in tone but in musical and lyrical ideas—because I think it makes for a tighter, more absorbing evening. *Sweeney Todd* is a very good example of that: the utilization of musical themes over and over again, but developed, not repeating. Very few people writing do this kind of thing. I don't how many are classically trained or if the material lends itself. I learned all of these compositional principles from [Milton] Babbitt, everything I'm telling you.

What it amounts to is, music exists in time, so how do you make it cohere? How do you make it more than just a set of add-a-pearls? And that's just as true with a three-minute song as it is with an hour-and-a-half opera, you know? I remember, we analyzed Mozart's Thirty-ninth to see how he held it together. Why is this *one* symphony? We're talking about different movements, so it isn't like he's using the same tune, because he's not, and yet there's a coherence. And, of course, *Wozzeck* and *Lulu* are great examples of that on the stage. Each one is one piece. And then there are of course the other kinds of operas, like *Carmen*, which is just twenty of the best tunes you've ever heard in your life, but they're twenty different tunes, you know? With a little fate theme that pops up every five minutes. But I like the idea of the kind of musicals I write, because they're so strong in the librettos, and because you really try to interest an audience in the story, as opposed to what musicals used to be, before Rodgers and Hammerstein ruined it for the rest of us.

And in the case of the Buñuel—

Yup. Buñuel. I'm still feeling my way, because the quality of the material—it isn't the kind of tight story that something like *Sweeney* or *Merrily We Roll Along* is. It's a series of vignettes, really. There are six main characters, and they interact, but there's very little plot. I mean, it's about a group of people trying to find a place to eat.

So the musical is actually from Buñuel's film *The Discreet Charm of the Bourgeoisie*?

The first act, yes. The first half is: They try to find a place to eat. The second act is *The Exterminating Angel*: They find a place to eat, and they can't leave.

This is something you've been thinking about for a long time, right?

Actually, it stems from a remark Hal Prince made in a cab once. We were looking out at night, coming back from the theater or something, and he was looking around Park Avenue on the way to the Upper-Middle East Side, and he said, "You know what the dominant form of entertainment is?

Eating out." [*Laughs.*] Because all the restaurants were lit up—it was about ten thirty in the evening, and that's what people were doing. They weren't going to the theater. They were eating! And I thought, "Gee, what an interesting idea." And I didn't immediately think, "Oh, that would make a musical." But somehow what happened was, David [Ives] and I started to write another show, and we bogged down and we aborted it for numerous reasons—and we had talked about Buñuel at one point. So that's how the idea arose. Dave was looking for something and I was too.

Do you have a bunch of things going at once?

No, no.

And has that always been the case for you?

Yes. I find it very useful to be only involved in one world. I don't know, do you write more than one piece at the same time?

I mean, I'm working on a book too, so I have to.

Oh, so you work on the book and then do a profile while you're still working on the book?

It's not ideal, but on the other hand, it takes so long to write a book, and money flies out the door . . .

Please, I understand the practical reasons.

It's harder.

What happens is, you get back to it, and you think, "Wait a minute, wait a minute, I had her going—no, she went into the bedroom."

Totally. There's a wonderful phrase from Thornton Wilder, who described literature as "the orchestration of platitudes"—meaning that a lot of writing fiction is about moving a person from here to there. And that's the stuff I always forget—like, "Oh, I already laid in this moment, and I gotta pay it off."

Yes, exactly. Or, "Wait a minute, she left the bedroom."

Exactly, exactly. So you do one at a time, and that's been true since . . . ?

Always, always, always.

Since *Gypsy,* or—?

Oh, since *West Side.* Well, since *Saturday Night,* which was my first attempt. I mean, I'm sure I've written an introduction to a book or something like that. But I don't think I've ever written a piece of music while I was writing a score for one thing. Certainly, whether it's the fact or not, the truth is the answer is no. I never do.

So when you have an idea that you think is pretty good, but you're working on something else, what do you do with the idea?

An idea for a show? Oh, I don't. Well, that's not quite true. The idea that we aborted was an idea I'd had for a long time. And I went to various playwrights—I went to Craig Lucas, I went to Terrence McNally—and they each were intrigued by it, but they didn't get what I had in mind. And then finally I asked David, and he got it right away.

And ultimately the issue was on your end or his end?

I'll tell you what the issue was: We started it, wrote it,

and then a show was done which had a similar idea and only lasted two days. It was not the same idea, but it was a similar idea. And then a movie came out, and it was also a similar idea. If I had gotten off my ass and done the work quickly, we would have beaten them to the punch, but we didn't.

Was it painful?

Yes, awful. Just terrible.

Where does the material go? Do you have an archive?

Before I write, I always spend time with the librettist, obviously, talking and talking and talking and talking—so we had talked, and David had written a scene, two scenes, and I wrote about two and a half songs. But those ideas and that music—I rarely—up until a few years ago, I had never re-used a trunk tune.

Did you call it "a trunk tune"?

Yeah, you have a trunk in the attic with all of your—some writers have a bottom drawer in the den. My trunk, unfortunately, is a briefcase. [*We laugh.*] A melody in *Bounce* was taken from a version of *Assassins*, for a song called "It's in Your Hands Now." But it's a very rare case. Music has just as much flavor for its purpose as prose does, so, you know, a tune that fits *Passion* is unlikely to be a tune that will fit the atmosphere of *Merrily We Roll Along*.

For you, which comes first, the music or the lyrics?

Oh, they come together.

Together?

[We joke about the wonderful exchange in Merrily We Roll Along:

*Interviewer: Now, when you do work together, I've always been
curious: Which generally comes first—the words or the music?*

Charley: Generally, the contract.]

Oh, sure. I mean, you get the idea for the song, you talk to
the librettist, and—if I could get a phrase that sort of sums
it up, you know, "It was just one of those things"—you can
start writing a lyric, and then the inflection of the *lyric* sug-
gests a tune. If you wrote down "It was just one of those
things," I don't know how *you'd* hear it, but *I* would hear
it, maybe, as "It was *just* one of those things." You might
hear this: "It was just *one* of those *things*." And that could
be another tune: "da-da-da-*dum*." Now we're talking about
conversational lyrics—there's a whole other kind of lyric
writing. It was essentially pop music for so many years—
the old pop music of the 1920s, '30s, '40s. But as dramatic
songwriting took over, Rodgers and Hammerstein, the kind
of thing we're talking about became more important: that
they should sound as if they're speaking, as opposed to just
singing, [*He sings.*] "Youuu are so beautiful."

When you have a conversation, are you hearing rhythms?
Yeah, quite often. And I'll tell you, Oscar [Hammerstein]
was—well, I won't say a pioneer at this, but, because *Oklahoma!* was such a big hit, everyone started to do this. I've
always been extremely critical of Larry Hart, but Oscar's
claim was that Larry Hart was the one who started to infuse

popular music with ordinary talk, street talk. That's true: If you look at songs prior to the 1920s, it's all artificial. The point is that he started to infuse popular songs with the kind of daily talk instead of fancy talk.

It kind of corresponds to what went on in poetry.
Yes! Oh yes, absolutely right. William Carlos Williams!

There's nothing more painful than picking up a volume of nineteenth-century verse and just thinking, They tried so hard.
Well, that depends—

I don't mean Tennyson. Tennyson is a genius.
Well, that's the whole point. Tennyson and Keats—they made artifacts that have nothing to do with contemporary speech. That was not what they were interested in. Poetry was about carving and decorating the language—and still saying something, but lots of rhymes, you know, all the artificial stuff.

[I mention having read through a book by the late nineteenth-century poet Francis Thompson and been bored by its stilted language.]

Listen, we can make parallels and analogies all night long, because that's what opera is to me. Opera, as opposed to musicals, has nothing to do with real life. Now, I know that when opera works for people, it's much bigger than real life, in the sense that you get real life the way you're supposed to out of artificial art.

Are there no operas that are exceptions to this?
Oh, of course.

Which ones?

Puccini, I think, was a master at psychological songwriting, and I believe his characters. And, if the story's interesting, I get interested in the story. However, outside of *Wozzeck*, I don't think I've ever seen an opera that sustained my interest all the way through. I mean my interest goes up and down, in and out. I prefer to listen to opera at home, because then I can just go from musical passage to musical passage, and I don't have to fill in with, uh, [*singing*] "Will you take out the garbage?" "No, I can't take out the garbage." [*Laughs*] Recitatif, to me, is the death of music. And you know I worship *Porgy and Bess*, you know that kind of opera which is much closer to the kind of musical theater that I write and was brought up on. And *Carmen* is except for its longueurs a really great story with songs as opposed to arias.

What about *Rigoletto*?

Verdi and I do not get along. Harmonically, he just drives me crazy—and that's just personal taste. I was brought up on movies, and, to me, Puccini is the kind of music that I enjoy. A lot of people find it overly fruity, and I don't . . . For me, the harmonies are what make music, and I love Puccini's harmonies, and I don't love Verdi's harmonies.

Is it that they're too obvious?

No, not at all. I don't think I could possibly explain it. It's just personal taste. Either you like parsnips or you don't like parsnips.

Do you find that your taste in music has changed through the years? In terms of popular music?

Well, I don't listen to much popular music. Even as a kid, I listened to movie music and classical music, and then when I got interested in the theater I listened to theater music.

So, like, the Beatles?

The Beatles are exceptional because they were so original and startling, but when I listened to others of their contemporaries I just wasn't as interested. And very little pop music is harmonically interesting—one of the exceptions being Radiohead, so I like to listen to Radiohead.

I've never really given them a full listen.

Well, if you're into harmony, they're certainly a lot more interesting than most of what goes on. But it's unfair of me to speak this way. I don't want to come off as somebody who disdains popular music. I just don't listen to it very often. First of all, it takes time. Secondly because I'm not in the car very often, you know, and I don't like rock concerts because I don't like that kind of crowded feeling.

Did you ever?

No. Well, when my dad took me to ball games, I liked that kind of crowd. But it's different when you're in the outdoors. Being in a large, enthusiastic crowd—more than enthusiastic, I mean, with a tendency to get out of control, because that's what the fun is—that frightens me. So I don't enjoy it.

You're a teenager in what decade?

In the forties.

So then, the music of that time—

Well, that's when I got interested in the theater. *Oklahoma!* is 1943. So starting then—

And how old were you in 1943?

Thirteen.

So, you were young.

Yeah, you said teenager! Prior to that I'd been playing classical piano, so I would listen to a good deal of classical music from the age of ten or eleven. But I listened to the pop music of the day because I was a movie bug, and so I'd hear all those movie songs.

But movie songs back then were their own weird genre. I mean, there were people who composed for—

Yeah, but they were related to the theater. You know, Rodgers and Hart were composing movie songs.

Really?

Oh, sure.

I was thinking of, like, Douglas Sirk—the background music that accompanies it.

Oh, the background music—yeah, that's a whole other thing. Background music I was into because all the back-

ground music was stolen from Strauss, and even in the 1940s,
noir films and Stravinsky. So, movie music was all part of the
so-called concert music for me. But, you know, they didn't
record scores in those days, so I only heard the music when
I went to the movies. As for pop music, I heard it because I
would listen to the radio, but I didn't seek it out. And you
know, there was no such thing as pop concerts. You went
dancing, but . . .

Did you do that?
  No.

You were not a dancer, ever?
  No, I'm a klutz as a dancer.

So when your mother moved you out to Bucks County—
  I was eleven.

I'm sorry not to know—
  That's alright. [*He's happy to tell the story again.*] The Hammersteins lived nearby, and they had a son my age, or maybe
a year younger, Jimmy. And I had no siblings, so Jimmy and
I became friends, and we would bicycle over to each other's
houses. I went to boarding school, but during the summer I
was there in Doylestown, and so was Jimmy. And the Hammersteins had a tennis court and they abutted a golf course,
so Jimmy and I cut through the fence, and we played the
eighth and seventh holes, and that sort of stuff.

And where did you go to boarding school?

I went to military school first. The New York Military Academy, in Cornwall-on-Hudson. It's right up from West Point—it's the little brother of West Point.

What was *that* like for you?

I loved it, because it was all ordered. My life was chaos—my parents split, and my life was completely disordered—so I loved the discipline. I thought it was great to have to be *there* at nine o'clock and *there* at nine thirty and *there* at ten o'clock.

And the uniforms, and the polish?

Oh no, the uniforms—that was boring, because you had to polish that stuff. I just remembered it was called Noxon. That was what you had to use to polish the brass. I was just in the lower school—I was there only from sixth through eighth grade—but I skipped, 'cause I was very good at school, so it was really only two years. It was just before high school.

Was this a decision that your parents made?

Yes. The place was *filled* with the sons of divorcées.

It was still unusual in that period.

I don't think so.

Moderately.

It was also very interesting, a lot of them were from around here—from New York City. A lot of Italian kids and a lot of Jewish kids.

And what did that lead to?

Nothing.

I just thought maybe it made for better eating. Or better singing. Or more sophisticated—

I just remember because I was always sort of interested in names and words, and I thought it was interesting.

And did you do musical theater there?

Oh no—there was no such thing.

Nothing?

No, no, no. I played the organ. They had, I think, the second-biggest organ in the state of New York. I think only Radio City Music Hall's was bigger. I think it was bigger than the Roxy's. And it had four manuals, and all the colored buttons, and my feet didn't quite hit the foot pedals, but I sort of stood up and played the organ there. And that was my only connection to music. I did it, really, for fun—it wasn't a course. It was the gadgetry of it. I wasn't taking piano. I wanted to play the toy.

But you'd already done piano as a smaller kid?

Yeah, yeah. Every nice, little upper-middle-class Jewish boy on the West Side took piano lessons, and I did, too.

This is a trivial question, but what would you play at a military academy? March music? Sousa?

No, no, no, no. The first piece I learned was "Aase's Death" from *Peer Gynt*. It's very easy to play because it's just slooow chords, sloooow chords. [*His voice rises to imitate the rising melody.*] And what else . . . I think I played a simple Bach prelude. I can't remember beyond that.

Were you giving concerts?

Oh no, no, no. There was a teacher, and I—it was an extra-curricular activity.

Were there other kids who were interested in music as well?

No, not that I remember.

So who was in the hall when you would play?

Nobody! It was a huge assembly room, and during the afternoons, I guess, when everybody was doing other things, I went in there. Obviously, I must have gotten permission. They must have said, "OK, those guys are making macramé, so you can play the organ."

And then high school?

Oh, for high school, I went to a prep school called George School.

I know that one—it's still around.

Oh, sure. Newtown, Pennsylvania. It was the oldest co-ed prep school in the country. It's Quaker. It's a Friends school.

And was that your dad or your mom's idea?

That was—let me think. How'd I get there?

Seems like a more sensible choice for a West Side boy.

I think probably because I was living in Pennsylvania with my mother, and Newtown was closer than Amherst or you know. I was there for four years.

Did you come into the city to hear bands and stuff?

No, again, you didn't go to hear bands—you're in the wrong generation. There was no such thing. If you wanted to hear a band, you went to one of the Broadway movie houses. You went to the Strand, where you saw a movie, a short, coming attractions, cartoons, and a band with a singer, and maybe even dancers. Or you went to Radio City Music Hall, where it was the same thing, except it was a more elaborate stage show. But the Strand, the Paramount, the Capitol, and each one—

I didn't realize they had live music.

Oh yeah. That's how Frank Sinatra got his start.

This isn't the era where Eddie Condon was around?

Oh, Eddie Condon was around. Now you're talking about jazz clubs, and I didn't go to any of those. If I went to a band at all—I only went because my father took me to the movies. Remember, in those days, you couldn't go to the movies unless you were with an adult.

Really?

Yeah. Until you were sixteen.

Any movie?

Any movie.

I didn't know that!

Well, actually there was an exception. Some of the neighborhood houses—like the Loews houses and the RKO houses—on Saturday matinees, you could go without a grown-up, but you had to sit in a special section with other kids and a nurse in a white uniform, who would wander up and down the aisles to be sure you weren't pulling some girl's hair or putting gum under the seats or peeing on the floor, or, you know, et cetera. But that was the only time a kid under sixteen was allowed into a movie house. I remember, my father took me to *The Cat and the Canary*, with Bob Hope—a scary movie—at the Paramount. And when Paulette Goddard was in bed and a clawed hand came out through a secret panel over her head to grab the necklace on her, I left and went to the bathroom 'cause I couldn't stand it, and I came back, and I was like, "Fuck, I missed it!" So the next day I played hooky and I stood outside the Paramount and asked a kind stranger, "Would you take me inside?—so I could see what happened to Paulette Goddard when the hand came down?"

How old were you, roughly, at this point?

I'd say thirteen, maybe.

Wow. And jazz was never an interest of yours?

No.

And what was your—?

Classical music and theater, eventually.

There's a lot of syncopated rhythms in jazz.

Well, yeah. But to this day, I like structure, and the whole idea of jazz is improvisatory. That's the fun of it, and that's the creative part of it. And I like to listen to jazz, but it never occurs to me to go and *pursue* a jazz concert. I enjoy it, but it's not—but then, it wouldn't occur to me to go hear Glenn Miller either. I went to hear Glenn Miller if there was a movie playing that I wanted to see.

But you actually liked to listen to jazz?

No. I say I *like* jazz. But I never put on a jazz record and I never went to a jazz club until I was much older, and somebody would take me because *they* wanted to go.

And your feeling was always, "It's fine"?

It's nice. It's fine. I say, it was nothing I wanted to pursue. I didn't avoid it, but I didn't go for it. And I didn't have any friends who were into jazz, so I never went to jazz.

But you were drawn to show music from a very early age.

That's a different kind of music.

No, I know. And you're drawn to show music from—

From meeting Oscar [Hammerstein].

Not before that?

Not particularly. I was drawn only to classical music, in terms of what I wanted to listen to. All my records—I spent my allowance on recordings—they were all the Romantic composers. Brahms, Rachmaninoff, Ravel—all the late nineteenth, early twentieth century.

Sibelius?

Oh yeah, Second Symphony—first time I heard that!—

Do you know the violin concerto?

Oh yeah. Well, I didn't get into the violin material until I was much older. I've never been a violin fan.

Oh my God. I should leave!

No, no, not at all! Because I got to them. It just never occurred to me to really buy a violin literature—I was into the piano. I bought every piano concerto that was available. And I remember tracking down—we're talking about now in the old Shellac days, where each record had only three minutes on a side—and I remember I read that there was a recording of a piano concerto, something Chinese—it was a very rare album by a Russian named Aaron Avshalomov, and I finally found that there was a copy in Shanghai, and I sent for it. It was a big deal to get it.

That's amazing. The thing must have weighed ten pounds, too.

Yeah, exactly—and the shipment came without being broken!

Those are the seventy-eights, right?

That's right. There was another thing, too. Have you ever heard of a Capehart? The Capehart phonograph was a console that played both sides of a Shellac record, and it had a mechanism: [*He uses his hands to mimic the Capehart mechanism with great affection. It reminds me of my own KLH Model Twenty-Plus.*] Here's the turntable, like this, and the record sat on the turntable ridge like that, and there was what looked like a music stand standing up this way, and you stacked the records here, and the thing would go down like that and go back up, and the record would play. This then would come back down and slide the record, so it came up here, and now the other side went down. And watching that happen—because it's gadgety—at the age of four, I loved it. And that was a status symbol. To have a Capehart in your house was like having a Steinway.

What gadgets give you similar pleasure today?

The iPhone and the computer but I'm very much of a neophyte on them. I'll tell you, if I was born a couple of generations later, I think I would have been a computer programmer. Because I've always been mathematically inclined, and I love what they do. I think Word is one of the great inventions of mankind. I'm absolutely astonished with that program.

What aspects?

Everything! How it does everything. How it keeps track of everything. And it's so simple to operate, once you learn what you can do. But I'm sure if I got into any of the other programs, I'd feel the same way. I just think programs for computers—man, they're just masterpieces!

So you enjoy sending emails, for instance?

No, no.

Because of the time?

Exactly. The gadget aspect of sending an email, yes—but no, I hate it. I try not to spend any time with a computer except for writing, and that means working.

You may have the discipline where you don't need this, but I recently downloaded a program that forcibly keeps you off the internet.

I don't have that problem.

You're able to stay off?

Yup.

It may be a generational thing, but the temptation to check your messages, emails, whatever, is constant.

Sure. I live with a guy who goes to bed with his iPhone, and the minute he wakes up—I would think naively, "Oh, he's looking at the news, at what Trump has done." Not at all! He's looking at Facebook, Face-fucking-Book. And to watch him maneuvering—I mean, like his entire generation, and certainly the younger generation—

But you admire the machinery?

I think if I'd been born two generations later, I'd be the same way. Because I'm easily addicted, and this is the kind of stuff that ordinarily I'd be addicted to. But because I didn't grow up with it, it doesn't interest me the way it does other people. I've never even been—I glanced over his shoulder once, but I've never seen Facebook. Apparently, I have sites on it, but I've never seen it, and I have no interest in seeing it. At my age, what I don't want to do is meet anybody else. I don't want to communicate with strangers, I don't want friends, I don't want to *friend* anybody or be *friended* by anyone. But if I were fifty years younger, it would be another matter.

So, for your social life, do you use the phone? Do you call people?

I used to enjoy being on the phone, but it's the same thing—I want to just be left alone.

It's amazing how much time people spent on the phone, isn't it? The phone never rings anymore!

Yeah, in my twenties, I'm sure you had to pick it out of my ear. You want to communicate with friends. You want a lot of people when you're young. And then eventually, if you settle down and have a family, then your circle becomes smaller, and then if you get old like me, your circle becomes *really* small.

Do you watch a lot of TV?

No, no. In fact, I watch no TV. Not that I have anything against it, but it takes time. I'm an old-movie buff, and by old movies I'm talking about my era: 1930s, 1940s.

So how do you get them?

I TiVo them, and then late at night I also watch—I like British murder mysteries. You know, polite, genteel, tea-cup murder mysteries. And like everybody else, I was a big *Breaking Bad* fan. I couldn't wait for each next episode. I find that there are so many good thriller series, and particularly from Britain. I don't know if you've seen *Happy Valley*, but oh, man, it was good. So that's what I watch late at night. I eat late at night because I'm like my father: I fall asleep after I eat. So if I want to get any work done, I don't eat until late, which is not very good. But while I eat, we watch a thriller series.

And how do you find the stairs here? Questionable decision to live in an entirely vertical townhouse!

[*Laughs*] At this age, I'm sorry. It was all fine until four or five years ago. Now I wish I had an elevator—it's really hard for me to climb stairs. It's not physical strength; it's balance. [*He describes the arduous process of climbing a staircase.*] Balance is one of the things that goes as you get older, you know—you have people falling all the time. Well, the reason they're falling is because their balance is gone. I find if I get up in the middle of the night to go to the john, I have to be real careful. If I just walk ordinarily, I may fall because I'm not sure where the step is, blah, blah, blah. That's one of the things that goes. Physical strength goes, muscle strength goes, and balance goes. And your brain goes. [*Laughs*]

Were you ever an exercise-type person?

No. I did a lot of athletics in prep school.

But after that?

Not as grown-up, no. Very lazy. Very sedentary.

You resisted those calls to go to the gym in the '60s, '70s, '80s?

There was a very good gym across the street, in my thirties

and forties, and I used to go there, because I thought to keep in shape, and it was across the street. Once they moved, I moved back to the couch.

You told me once that you'd "lived your entire life in twenty blocks." Have you been here for much of that time?

Oh yeah, since 1960. It's the house that *Gypsy* built.

And you never left? It was just perfect for you?

Nope. You know, look behind you—that garden out there . . . there are twenty gardens out there made into one big garden. It's unique in New York, I think. I used to serve on the garden committee. There's a little community in these gardens. When I moved here, Katharine Hepburn was next door, and on the other side was Ruth Gordon and Garson Kanin. This was theater row down here, in this corner of the garden.

So you were trading up when you bought in here. How old were you?

I was thirty years old when I bought the house.

You were a boy!

A boy? Well, yeah. I'd had two shows, *West Side* and *Gypsy*. And *Gypsy* is the one that I got enough income that I could put a down payment on the house with a loan from the bank. My father cosigned the loan. He was a dress manufacturer, a very successful one—well, I shouldn't say *very* successful. At the end of his life the business completely collapsed, and he died in a lot of debt.

Was it called Sondheim . . . ?

Yeah, Herbert Sondheim, Inc. In fact, it was a nice moment a few years ago—there was a Fashion Institute exhibition up at the Met, and one of the dresses that was shown was worn by Jackie Kennedy.

Oh, so he was prominent.

He was quite well known. He was the CEO. My mother was a designer, and he was the man who—

Were they couture?

No, no. He sold to Bergdorf, to Saks—that was the level. It was middle-priced dresses, not haute couture.

But those were the great stores.

Yeah, exactly. I grew up in the model's room down on Seventh Avenue, 530 Seventh Avenue. And four times a year, I guess, he would have a showing with the buyers—but it was just an office, maybe three times the size of this room. This was not, like, Fashion Week at Bryant Park.

Dad was constantly entertaining buyers. So it was a great boon for him when I started to have a hit show of any sort, because he could—

Take a pair.

You got it. On the other hand, he would have preferred me to write shows like *As the Girls Go* instead of *West Side Story*. [*Laughs*]

What was *As the Girls Go*?

As the Girls Go was what they used to call "a tired business-man show." It starred a comic called Bobby Clark, who was one of the big comics, and it was a lot of pretty girls, and the opening was a number called "As the Girls Go," and in come twenty chorus girls, and that was people's idea of a musical.

Did any of this give you an interest in the costume side?

I have no visual gift at all.

Did either of your parents play the piano?

My mother was entirely visual; my father played by ear. He would go to a Broadway show and come home and pick the tunes out on the piano. And when I was a tiny kid I would sit on the piano bench, and he would put my little hand on his right hand, and I would play the piano with him.

Were you a good classical pianist?

Very good right hand; left hand, awful. I'm just very, very right-handed at everything. I'm very right-handed at picking things up.

You can't be a great pianist with only the right hand.

But I didn't want to. I had no ambition.

You didn't want to be the next—

I certainly did not. When I was in prep school, I would give recitals around Pennsylvania, sometimes a solo and some-times with my music teacher playing the second piano. One day, I was playing at our main rival—it would have been called something like Lancaster Friends—I was playing the Chopin F-sharp Minor Polonaise, which has an ABA structure. I finished the A, and I was on automatic pilot, and I thought, "Oh, fuck, I don't know what comes after the A." And so, in a panic, I went right back to the beginning of the A, and then finished the A.

And then?

The audience applauded. And I thought, "If they don't know, there's no reason for me to play the piano in public." They had no idea they'd been cheated of one-third! [*Laughs*]

How old were you?

Fifteen. And the music teacher did want to groom me for a piano career.

Did your parents ever want you to be, like, a lawyer?

No. I think Dad wanted me to be in the dress business, but he never pushed. My mother was a designer for my father, and then they split when I was eleven. She then worked for a well-known designer and then she became an interior decorator—she married a guy on the Coast—and she decorated some homes out there, some celebrities.

What year did she pass away?

Ah, my answer will amuse you. She passed away the night that *Merrily We Roll Along* opened in Leicester, England, 'cause that's where I was. George Furth and I rewrote the show and finally got it the way we wanted it, and we opened it in Leicester, and the phone rang just before the show began. And the mayor of Leicester, England, was coming to see the show, and this was in an upstairs office, and I got the news that she had passed away—she was in a nursing home—and I got into the elevator with the director, and he said, "Are you OK?" I said, "Oh yeah, my mother just died." The elevator doors at that point opened, and there was the mayor, and the director was, I think the word is gobsmacked. He was staring into the middle distance. "Yeah, my mother just died. Oh, Mr. Mayor, so nice to see you!" [*Laughs*]

She lived long enough to see her son as the glamorous person she would have liked you to be.

Oh yeah, don't think she didn't play off the celebrity. There was a big, big benefit—it must have been 1973—this benefit was held at the Shubert Theatre, and there were a number of celebrities. And afterward there was a party. My mother's nickname was Foxy, because her maiden name was Janet Fox. And she came over because I was sitting with Lenny Bernstein, and just to be polite, as she came over, he looked up and said to her, "Foxy, aren't you proud?" She said, "He belongs to the ages!"

[*Laughing*] What did you do?

Blushed, you know, changed the subject. Ugh! She gave a cocktail party once—here's a mama story. [*Laughing*] I hated all her cocktail parties, but she wanted me there—she wanted to show me off. She said, "I got a present for you," and she had bought a little gold keychain. It was a keychain with a charm on it, with a little gold book with the names of my shows, each one with a single adjective that had been applied to it. It was a nice adjective. And I looked and said, "Mom, *Anyone Can Whistle* isn't here." She said, "THAT WAS A FLOP!"

[*Laughing*] God, she was relentless!

What we call a pistol, yeah.

All these years later, it all feels OK in retrospect?

She was so outrageous that now I can tell funny stories.

But it hurt at the time.

It's not that it hurt. It was an annoyance. She kept trying to blackmail me, and, you know, "I'm dying, I'm dying." I'll tell you a lot of funny stories about that. She was terrible at it. Always got caught in the lie. And she milked me for money—she *stole* money from me. I still would like her to suffer. [*Laughs*] But I don't think about her. She was completely exorcised, because I've told so many people about what a horror she was, and I've told so many funny stories that I laugh at them now.

She's become material.

Yes, that's very good. Exactly. It's a help, because you're still getting back at them, but you're doing it in a way that doesn't irritate you.

And whereas your father—where is he sitting with you?

Oh, I liked him a lot. But, you know, I went to a shrink—to two shrinks—and what became apparent was that he was a swell guy, but he left me in the lion's den. He couldn't live with that monster, and he fell in love with another lady, so why the fuck shouldn't he leave? On the other hand, it wasn't so good for the kid. So if you were he, what would you do? He was not careless about me—he was always trying to make things nice and help—but she wouldn't talk to him.

She made him suffer for the break.

Oh yeah. And she tried to poison me against him, but she was so rotten at it, the more she tried to poison me, the more I liked him.

She was a theatrical figure in a way.

Yup. And the other side of her is that she was talented. She was very good at what she did. I'm told she was a good dress designer. She was sought after.

[We talk about mid-century American design and then I change the subject.]

Just getting to work habits: This show that you're working on now, for instance—what is the process? Do you sit at the piano? Look at the sky?

Are you talking about writing music? I write longhand, because a lyric is only sixty words. Actually, I'm lying, because in the last couple years I've started to sketch lyrics on the computer.

How does one sketch lyrics?

Well, it's sort of free association.

*[Sondheim excuses himself to go up the stairs to use the bathroom.
"It will only take me a half hour to get up the stairs," he says. He
tells me that if he's gone too long, to "send one of the dogs up" after
him. As he leaves, he tells me a funny Mary Rodgers anecdote
about a bathroom that used to be on the first floor and is now a
closet: she was afraid people would hear her peeing so she always
ran the water. He makes a big whooshing noise for the water sounds.
He invites me to knock on the kitchen door if I want any more to
drink. I thank him.*

*When he returns, a woman on his staff offers us each another glass
of wine. I tell him I don't want to wear him out but if he's OK, we'll
continue. He says he is, and I gingerly ask about the timing of
Buñuel; he says he is unsure.]*

I expected over the last month for them to be dogging me
because I'm so far behind but I haven't heard from them.
Maybe they've lost interest. [*He pauses, maybe briefly hoping
this improbability is true.*] The general idea is next spring.

Spring of '18?
  '18.

Then you've got to get going! Sorry!
  You're telling me!

**If this is unpleasant don't—[*I decide to go forward with my
question.*]—How many songs have you got written for the
Buñuel?**
  I've written . . . seven.

Wow!

Oh no. C'mon now. Theoretically, that's the first act, so I'm starting the second act, which would be at least as many, I think.

How many songs are in *Sweeney Todd*?

Sweeney Todd has many more songs than most shows. There are more than twenty-three—twenty-four, maybe. An ordinary musical score is about fourteen—you know, *Merrily We Roll Along*, *Company*.

And you see all the revival productions in New York?

I work on them.

You work on them—that's what I thought. So, the 2017 production of *Pacific Overtures*—that wasn't actually all of the original *Pacific Overtures*, right?

It was cut. There was one song cut: "Chrysanthemum Tea," which was something that John Doyle, the director, and John Weidman [the book writer] decided, and then sent to me. Because it's a vignette that does not carry the action forward, really—if anything, it slows it up. It's part of the plot, but it's not necessary. So that's what we call an unnecessary song. But that was part of the idea of the show, you know.

It was?

Yeah. Hal wanted a Kabuki show, and Kabuki theater is not one continuous story. Kabuki theater is much closer to a vaudeville, in which you have, you know, this scene, that scene, this scene, that scene: a comic song, a dramatic scene, a swordfight, an acrobat, a dog. And that's what Hal wanted. So it had a patchwork quality. But to do it down here, it seemed to both Johns that it was necessary to tighten it and hold an audience's attention, because they had none of the visual spectacle that Hal had, and blah, blah, blah. So that was cut, and then little bits of other things were cut.

Did the production please you?

Yeah, I liked it.

I thought it was wonderful.

The best production was a Japanese production. In 1990, I got an award called the Praemium Imperiale.

Well!

Yeah, it's this sort of Nobel Prize given by the Japan Art Association—they give one in each discipline of architecture, sculpture, painting, music, and theater. And it happened at the time that there was a production at the Japanese National Theatre of *Pacific Overtures*, which was directed by a young director there. And Weidman and I went to see it, just out of curiosity, and we were—I hate the phrase—blown away. We were blown away. And I did something I've never done before or since: I promoted it. I came back to the United States and I called the Kennedy Center, and I said—I can't remember who I knew down there—"This production is worth importing. It's really spectacular." And they did. And then I promoted it at Lincoln Center, and we did it in Avery Fisher Hall.

What year was that?

1991 or '92? I don't know.

You did it in full costume?

Oh, they brought the whole production over. The whole Japanese production: the Japanese cast, the Japanese director. The one thing they couldn't do is they had a spectacular finale, and it was too expensive to bring over here, because it involved a lot of projectors, and so on. And the *hanamichi*—it's that runway—it went right from the back of Avery Fisher Hall down to the stage. It was spectacular. It was shoulder-height of the sitting audience, and that's where the gods came in in the original Japanese theater. But in *Pacific Overtures*, it's where the high muck-a-mucks come, both the court and the Americans. But the whole production—I have a tape of it—it's in Japanese, and there are no subtitles, but if you're a fan, you'll know what's going on. Wait till you see it. Man, it is something.

So they brought it to the US in Japanese?

Yes, exactly. They just imported it. The way they import stuff at BAM.

Were you worried this time that by having no orchestra and costume—?

What do you mean no orchestra? That orchestra sounded great!

Ah, I'm confusing it with *Sweeney Todd*.

Oh, that's different. That's an orchestra of three; this is an orchestra of seven. It was wonderful. A small orchestra in a small place is like a big orchestra in a big place, only it's crystal: it couldn't have been clearer. And I thought the orchestration of *Sweeney Todd* was *brilliant*. I thought those three instruments playing that stuff was just atmospheric and—have you seen it?

Yeah, I went.

Didn't you think that it was terrific?

Yeah, I did, but I saw the original so long ago.

It's a very small place, and it's all in your face and in your lap, and I thought these three instruments absolutely conveyed all the atmosphere and mystery and comedy.

Who thought of rescoring it that way?

Oh, that's—don't you know how that production started?

Well, it began in England, I know, but I don't know the details.

It began in a section of London, the equivalent of Greenwich Village, which is called Tooting, and there is a Tooting Arts Club, which is run by this enterprising lady whose name is Rachel Edwards. And she does site-specific theater, and she goes hat in hand to the community and says, "This production is going to cost two hundred pounds. Would you contribute ten pounds?" And they do. And she had the idea of doing *Sweeney Todd* at this pie shop, because it's the oldest pie shop in London. She went to the owners, and she said, "Could we have your pie shop at night?" And the owner said, "Yes, after six o'clock, it's yours." And the pie shop was smaller than the average musical theater, and so where're you gonna put the orchestra? So then she got a director and a music director, and he said, "I'll orchestrate it for upright piano and cello and a wind instrument."

And at what point do they come to you and go like, "We have this idea"?

Ah, they didn't. I found out about this. All they have to do is license it—musicals are licensed, most of them, by MTI, which is Music Theatre International.

So you don't even necessarily know about a production?

That's correct. If they want to do anything to it, like, "We want to cut this, we want to add this," then they have to get permission from MTI. Then MTI calls me and says, "They would like to cut this and add this," and then I say yes, no, or in between.

In this case, would they have had to ask you . . . ?

In this case, they didn't ask me, because nothing was changed.

Well, they reorchestrated it.

Ah, that's different. You can do it with a piano if you want. Unless you want to rent the orchestrations. If you want to rent the orchestrations, then I think you have to use what they give you—I'm not sure about that. But you don't have to. You can put it on in your high school with a piano as long as you don't change the music.

What else do you have coming up this coming fall?

I have a lot going on in England. There is gonna be a production of *Company* with a female Bobby, directed by Marianne Elliott, who may be the most brilliant director alive.

Do you know what month—?

There is a tentative schedule but I've been avoiding it because I've got to do some rewriting, because it isn't just a
matter of changing pronouns. I've got to rewrite some songs.
We've had numerous conversations. I'm just, you know, in
my usual way, I'm way behind on everything, and my pri-
orities are Buñuel. As I speak to you, I'm ready to commit
suicide.

*[He tells me the story of how he was convinced Elliott's female
Bobbie version would work. The key was a young man who watched a
workshop in England and told the production team, "I never heard of
this show before. You mean, it worked with a man!"]*

What sort of changes have you said no to?

Well, John Tiffany, who directed *Harry Potter and the Cursed
Child*—a really good director—wanted to do a gay male
version of *Company*. So we had a reading of that about a
year and a half ago, and I thought it didn't work at all, and
I said no.

What didn't work?

It just felt forced. The only scene, curious enough, that
seemed to work was Bobby and three girls on the park
bench, as Bobby and three *guys* on the park bench. The rest
of it seemed—it just wasn't written for it. As a friend of mine
said, George Furth is really J. D. Salinger. His ear for the
way people talk—and, because he was an actor, he *really*
understands character instinctively. He's one of those playwrights who write two lines, and you know who to cast.
If you saw people audition, you'd say, "That's the guy that

George wrote." Because his writing is *so* character specific. And that includes gender. He knows the way guys talk and the way girls talk and there's a difference. That sounds like male chauvinism but there is.

But you could flip Bobby?

Well, Bobby is another matter, because Bobby is a cipher. At least Marianne's point is that the problems the Bobbys of the 1970s faced are similar to the problems women today face.

I'm trying to think about what that would imply. He's a cipher, right?

That's it, yep. Everyone else is a character, and Bobby is the vacuum in the middle. And there's a reason he's a vacuum. He's somebody who soaks up and bottles up, and theoretically what he does at the end of the show is grow up and become somebody. That's the idea. The show either works or not, but that's the notion: that he learns from his friends to be a person. In fact, it's really like he's graduating at the end. When I came in to help direct a production down in Washington, in 2002, that was my metaphor to the cast. I said, "You are helping this boy grow up. Think of it that way throughout the show—that is what you're doing. And at the end, when you say, 'Happy birthday, Bobby,' it really means, Congratulations." And that's what I think the show is.

Right. So you're gonna rewrite—

I'll have to rewrite quite a lot of stuff. You've got to change tone.

Is there a line you're thinking—

No, no . . . I've made notes, but it's song by song and scene by scene. It's a lot.

Was it more than you meant to undertake when you said yes?

Yes. Yes, it is.

That's the problem with reediting one's old work.

That, and I don't like to go back to my old stuff, but the fact is, the reason I'm doing it is Marianne Elliott. I saw a lot of her work before *War Horse*, and I've always thought she was one of the best directors in the English language. So to work with her, I'll do this. I'll try it.

Whose musicals do you like to see nowadays?

I don't go to musicals.

You don't?

I don't.

Because you go to the theater a lot.

No, I don't!

Every time we're in touch, you're like, "I'm trying to get to a curtain by seven." That's robust!

Well, curiously, that's a coincidence. I've seen maybe four things this season.

What've you seen?

Oslo, which killed me—which shattered me.

So I should go?

I'll tell you what my reaction was. For three quarters of the evening, I thought, "This is one of those plays that's boring but interesting." And then at the end it adds up. It's not that something startling happens, but it adds up. And the last five minutes, I was shaking and sobbing. I cannot tell you why, but it was one of the most emotional experiences I've ever had in the theater. Usually I've had experiences like that at *The Miracle Worker*, where you *know* that she's gonna say "waa waa" and you're gonna be in pieces. Nothing happens here, except the world happens. I was completely knocked out. So yeah, I certainly suggest that.

Wow. So you saw that—what else?

What else . . . I haven't seen anything else that's impressed me as much. I haven't seen the new musicals.

Are there people who it would interest you to see writing music?

This is a subject that's taboo. Because if I say anybody, it hurts other people's feelings that they *weren't* mentioned, or if I criticize someone—so I just don't give opinions on anybody alive.

I was just thinking whether you felt that you had had any heirs.

I don't think that way.

You don't think that way?

No, I don't. Certainly, the received wisdom is that I've had a lot of influence on a lot of people, and sometimes I hear it. But you know, we all have influence.

[I press him to talk about specific shows whether pro or con but he declines.]

There's a lot to see. When you get to off Broadway, you gotta keep up, or you ain't gonna keep up.

That's the problem, yes. Off Broadway is the stuff where my interests lie, and I read about it. I'm sure there's stuff on Broadway I would like, but at the moment . . . I haven't gone down the list, but I will.

Do you go to London to see stuff?

Not to see stuff. I go to London, and *then* I see stuff. I get there about once a year for work, and I usually try to stay three or four days so I can see three or four things.

Is there a city you travel to for pleasure?

No.

Was there ever?

No. I like traveling once I go, but getting off my ass is . . .

But you were never—I'm just trying to think, in the seventies—

Well, I did go to various places.

I just thought maybe London in the '60s.

No.

Or Paris in the '50s.

Nah.

Or Fez in the '90s—

Sorry, no. That's not me. I'm *much* more provincial by nature.

And there's nowhere you wished you lived?

I love New York!

Our conversation confirmed what I had suspected: what Sondheim talked about most contentedly was how the hat was made—tricks of the hat-making trade, famous haberdashers he had known, notable hat design failures. The subject was just personal enough, and while it was partly about craft it was really ultimately about human interactions. As a result our conversation had been absorbing and fluid. It had also helped that I said less this time. Uninterrupted by mine, his conversation—really more of a flexible, redirectable lecture—stood on its own. I had learned a lot and of course enjoyed myself and he clearly had too.

I had done enough reading by now that I also knew things about him that helped me step outside our back-and-forth to see him more clearly. Some were trivial: While at Camp Androscoggin, he'd been given extra milk as a weight supplement. Some were amusing: When he was composing *Company*, Katharine Hepburn banged on his garden door and told him to pipe down. Some were intriguing: According to Meryle Secrest's 1998 biography, Sondheim liked to compose high because it helped him get a first draft of his lyrics out. But the fine-tuning he did sober. He had taught himself to love Bach but didn't like Mozart. It was the lush romantics he most related to. (At least this was true in the 1970s.) He had seen the musical *The Wiz* six times and loved it ("Everything just worked so well, even if it's not my kind of music," one audience member remembered him saying at a talk in New York, or at least saying something to this effect). He'd once wanted to make a musical out of *Groundhog Day*. I would have thought the whole *Saturday Night Live* gestalt would have left him cold, so I guessed what drew him was the repeating narrative structure. I'd also read in Secrest's biography that Sondheim had sought therapy in the mid-sixties after having an unhappy affair with a young man on the administrative staff of *Do I Hear a Waltz?* He added to Secrest: "I can't say it was love." And I made a fun discovery that afternoon in his house, on a visit to pee (all that wine). He had a book by the toilet with the title *The Playful Brain: The Surprising Science of How Puzzles Improve Your Mind* and, beside it, a half-done crossword puzzle.

Where was all this leading though? All these partial revelations about dedication to craft or repressed Eros, out-of-town fiascos and just-in-time epiphanies? Was I actually getting closer to answering the question of how whatever was true about him had molded him into such an astonishingly creative being? That's, in the end, the treasure everyone who ever interviewed Sondheim was searching for, and I was no different.

TRAVELING COMPANY

SEPTEMBER 2017

"Sadness is the necessary part."

After the PEN event, I'd ordered a copy of *Anyone Can Whistle* to see what had cost Sondheim his epaulets. The CD came, starring Angela Lansbury. Was it the right one? "It's the only OBC," he replied, using the acronym for Original Broadway Cast, and said next time I was over he would let me take a few things from the CD closet. I could hardly wait for this—I was sure there were treasures rarer than Avshalomov on his shelves.

I had told Sondheim at the end of our last interview, that I would be traveling with my son in Europe for a while. He told me to call him when I got back. But in keeping with my wedding guest notion, I waited a bit longer before suggesting another meeting. I was careful not to hold off too long, perpetual anticipation being a delicate art, as one of his characters sings somewhere. He answered that he would be at his summer house in Connecticut, but I should visit him there, he wrote with curious stiffness, to "help familiarize you with my other life venue." He cautioned; "two hours at most (I'd prefer one to one-and-a-half). I really have to work." Afterward, I told him, I would go on and see Twain's last home, which was nearby.

This meeting—though I did not know it then—was to be the culmination of our relationship. I would finally close that gap between my job as interviewer and my goal to be a listener. For awhile, we would be just two people talking. It would feel as if nothing could not be asked or said. I would leave with every expectation that there would be more such moments to come. But as good as I was getting at understanding how to be with Sondheim, I wasn't aware of all the booby traps I should be looking out for.

On a late summer day, I drove across the Tappan Zee and up to Roxbury. Sondheim had mentioned that he had taken refuge at his summer house because this was the middle of U.N. week, during which his neighborhood in Manhattan was unlivable. This area—Litchfield County in northwest Connecticut—was by contrast ostentatiously pleasant, with its restored barns and covered bridges. I parked my car in front of a studio building and walked past massive bushes to the front of the main house. I knock, hear a hello and let myself in. Two dogs bound at me like a long-lost member of the pack. Sondheim waits inside the house in blue pants and a yellow souvenir T-shirt from the Dominican Republic. We stop in the kitchen, which is spotless, with a range with red handles, a very clean counter, and a cupboard with a mug from *Sunday in the Park* with "Art Isn't Easy" written on it. It's just a container for coffee, I'm pretty sure, not an ironic gesture. (When I get home I order myself one online and, soon after, accidentally drop it.)

There is no staff here, no one to prepare the drinks. We are alone. Sondheim is the host.

Can I get you anything?

Sure. What are you serving?

[We both settle on something nonalcoholic.]

This is beautiful! Those are some serious rhododendrons you have out front.

[He tells me he doesn't know the names of flowers.]

[*To the dogs*] I know, you smell dog treats! [*To their fond owner*] Remind me of the poodles' names?

Addie and Willie—named after the Mizner brothers. Addie is a girl, and Willie is a boy. That's Willie, the larger of the two.

[This reminds me of Nemo, the rescue Sondheim had an indirect role in bringing into our lives.]

I'll tell you, I'm having dog problems. Our puppy is so spoiled that when I leave the house, he just howls.

Oh no. You have to just . . .

What do you do?

Well, first of all, leave your tears for the driveway. [*Laughs*]
That's very good advice, because separation anxiety—I suffer from it as well as the dogs. I understand what that's about.

Do you suffer from it with regard to the dogs?

Yes, a little bit.

Well, everybody understands what they're feeling.

*[We start walking through the house, past renovated-looking rooms.
There are gates to keep the dogs out or in.]*

So, did you work successfully this morning?

No.

No? Is that when you try to work, in the mornings? Or is it all day?

All day. I try to get interested in work and then I try to work.
And you've been to Twain?

**I just had too much to do this morning. I had to drop off my kids at
school, and . . .**

Remind me where you live?

I'm in Montclair—in Jersey

Oh my God! I forgot. That's a long journey.

**No! It was a good drive. And I'm going to stop by Twain's final
house, which he bought—you're going to love this—at the
suggestion of his biographer—**

Oh my God.

—who lived nearby. [*Laughs*]

That's funny! Where *had* he been?

He had this magnificent house in Hartford. It was bizarre—
it looked like a huge steamship. And Twain couldn't really
afford that, because he spent all his money investing in these
unsuccessful typesetting machines . . .

Oh right! He loved technology. He was famous for that.

Yeah! And so he has to sell this place, and then he tours Europe,
makes all of this money lecturing, pays off his bills, and then his
biographer says, "I have a huge piece of land in Redding." And he
buys right up the hill! It was really ill-considered.

[*Laughing*] And was he happy there?

He was! [*I think about this a bit harder.*] You know—it's life, right?
He thought he was going to have these glorious final years, but
one of his daughters died of epilepsy—

Oh God, oh God, oh God.

And he was certain his staff was stealing from him.

Actually that's in a movie. This Fredric March movie called
The Adventures of Mark Twain.

This house burned down after he died, but they rebuilt a similar
version. I just want to get a feel for the landscape.

The reason is that you're a Twain fan, or that you're writing
about it?

I'm writing a Twain book. It's a pleasure to write but I put it off, I put
it off, I put it off . . .

Don't we all? That's what pleasures are for!

I know, you're probably right. Alright, so, we can keep moving?

[We wind up in a long narrow room. Sondheim sits in an easy chair with his back to the view of sun-lit gardens and pretty fields outside.]

[*Beginning with my customary apology*] Let's do our thing. I'll stay an hour and a half or thereabouts. Whatever you can do. And then I'll go down the hill to Twainland.

[I notice an intriguing contraption—some sort of ship-friendly furniture—and ask if it's a copy or replica.]

It's not, I don't think, an original, as they say. It was manufactured in the nineteenth century. It's for ships. The superstructure comes off, but everything else folds in.

Wow!

It becomes a table for maps and things like that. It's for the captains. And it was invented for Hamilton.

Really?

Lord Hamilton.

Oh, not Hamilton the subject of stage and screen?

. . . or maybe it was Nelson. It might have been Nelson. Anyway, it was invented for a British admiral of some sort in the early nineteenth century. It's a manufactured object.

That's so cool. Where did you find it?

I have this friend Burt Shevelove, with whom I wrote some shows. He'd always wanted to live in London, and he moved there after the success of *Forum*. He's an antiqueophile—not so much fine antiques, but curious antiques. And every time he would find something weird, if he didn't have room for it himself, he would wire me and send me a picture and ask if I wanted it. I don't look for those things myself, but I can tell you all the stores in London that he used to take me to when I would go over there. I got a lot of interesting stuff.

It's good to have a friend like that.

Yup. And I *love* trick furniture.

Do you have other trick furniture?

Yeah, I have an orrery. I have two orreries, matter of fact, both of which he found, which are very hard to find.

I'm sorry, what's—

Lord Orrery invented—or, sorry, he *commissioned* the invention of a model of the universe—again, early nineteenth century. I'll show you later. They are very hard to find outside of museums.

So they are models of . . . ?

Of the planetary world as they knew it in those days.

Oh, wow.

And they are usually on clockwork mechanisms. The one I got from London was electrified, and it was clockwork. But I also have a table model. Come on, I'll show you.

I'll take some photos so I can describe things later, if that's OK.
I don't know why I was so slow to get an iPhone. For this kind of
work, there is nothing like it on this planet.

Yeah, it's perfect.

So, you know, these are free-form chats where we dart up and
back and around, but I wouldn't mind starting with—

Any free forms you want!

We saw each other, what, a couple months ago? So presumably
you've been working on Buñuel—

Slowly. I went to London a couple weeks ago to tend to
a production of *Follies* at the National Theatre, which I
went to for dress rehearsal, a couple previews. It opened last
week.

What did you think?

It's great!

I wish I could see it.

Oh boy, it is something. It's Imelda Staunton as Sally. It's
a really good production. And for an interesting reason, I
think: the director has never directed a musical before. He
was head of the Royal Court, so he has done lots of Shake-
speare, lots of contemporary plays—but because of that, he
treated this as a play, and of all the musicals I have written,
this is the one that needs a play director more. It's really, you
know, it's a pretentious word to use, but for lack of a better
one, it's Chekhovian. Because nothing happens on the surface and everything happens underneath. All the action is
internal. And even though they sing their little hearts out . . .

Are you going to shoot me?

Pardon? [*Sondheim has some sort of lethal-looking heavy-gauge gadget in his hand that he seems to be aiming at me.*]

What is that?

[*He examines it.*] I think it's a nutcracker but I'm not sure. This is just another thing Shevelove wished on me. He used to get stuff and then ask me if I knew what they were.

[*I take it from him and read what's written on it, "American Bulldog Bootjack."*]

That's what it is. It's a bootjack! It's to help pull on your boots. I just like objects.

Me too. OK ... "Chekhovian and everything happens under the surface...."

So, he's the perfect director for it. It's very good to look at, but the triumph is in the casting. [Elia] Kazan said eighty percent of direction is casting, and he was right.

What do you mean by that? I was actually listening to the original cast album on the way up.

Well, the thing is, there are twenty-three songs in the score, which leaves very little room for the book writer to do what he's supposed to do, which is called establish character. So all characters need to be established—of course the songs help establish them—but in the dialogue, you know, it's a few lines apiece, and I'd say the longest scene between two people is probably a page, or a page and a half. So it needs actors who bring personality onto the stage, so you understand something about them immediately. In the original, John McMartin gave what is one of my favorite, if not my favorite, male performances in a musical ever. He came onstage, and the minute he opened his mouth you *knew* he was a broken man. A lot of that had to do with the quality of John's voice and his physicality, which was also slightly bent, but the point is, you knew who he was right away, even though he was dressed elegantly in a black tie, and he was a commanding presence, and he had been in the U.N., and that sort of thing. Right away you knew something inside was broken. Same thing with Dorothy Collins: she came on, and you knew that she was an unhappy southwestern housewife just by the quality of the voice, and the costume. You need that in a show like *Follies*, because you don't get a chance to get to know these people. They come on, they sing something, and then they are offstage while other people take over. Because the show not only has twenty-three songs, but it's got a passel of subordinate characters, each of whom come on and interrupt the proceedings. [*He sips his soda water.*] Anyway, I made my point.

No, no, it's interesting.

And the result in this case is a triumph, because the audience gets to know who these people are right away and be carried along by them emotionally. The whole show is—I'll give you a quote. Peter Brook came on Saturday and said it was the best piece of musical theater he'd ever seen, and one of the best pieces of theater he had ever seen. That's a high compliment. As a friend of mine said, "From the guy who directed *Irma la Douce*." That's a nice bitchy remark!

[We discuss Sondheim's many commitments— "Moi?" he jokes. He complains they are slowing his work down. We discuss the London production of Company *with a female Bobbie.]*

I like taking chances, but it's really Marianne Elliott's baby.

[We discuss some more of Sondheim's coming obligations.]

So, on to Buñuel . . .
Byoon-well.

[I ask what the schedule on the show is now.]

They're shooting for late spring rehearsals which would mean fall opening. Shooting for . . . Hello I've just begun the second act.

But at this point, you've done the first act of Buñuel. You even workshopped it, right?
We had a reading. A reading is eight people sitting in chairs with scripts in their hands and then standing up and singing when it comes time to sing, with an invited audience. No staging. A workshop is minimal staging, but a staging, nonetheless. You get up and you go kiss her over there, and then she gets up, and she goes and shoots him over there. Whereas in a reading, you go "mwah" [*a kissing sound*], and she goes "BANG!"

Does that mean what you have of the first act is comparable to the first draft of a book?
Yes! The first draft. There is a complete score and a complete act, but I want to add and tweak. Second act, there is

a complete draft of the book, and I've just begun the score.

This is all complicated by the opera that is about to open at the Met. There is a composer in his early forties, who is one of probably two or three leading composers in Britain today, whose name is Thomas Adès. He has written an opera of *The Exterminating Angel*, which will open at the Met in October. None of this is a surprise, 'cause we had numerous communications with the Buñuel estate about the rights: they have granted him the opera rights and granted us the musical theater rights. They didn't know the difference, but we educated them. [*Laughs*] And then I talked to Adès about it, and I said, "Listen, I hope you don't think this is in any way competitive, because I can assure you, the treatments will be different." Adès is a master of orchestration—the orchestration for this opera is gigantic, wonderful, and weird—and the opera got rave reviews in both Salzburg and London, where it was done a month or two ago.

Will you listen to it?

No. I will go see it, but I probably will not go see it before I finish what *I'm* writing. I'm not sure.

Really? You're able to—

Oh yeah, because it's chalk and cheese. I mean, what he writes and what I write are just entirely different. His is real opera, with a great deal of very high singing, and spectacular orchestral effects, and a large cast. And he's only doing *The Exterminating Angel*. He's got twenty-four in his cast. Our version of *The Exterminating Angel* is the second act and only has eight people, so there is a big difference . . .

I would have shit my pants!

[*He pauses, wondering if he is as convinced as he sounds.*] If I were thirty-five years old, I think it would upset me a lot more. But at this age, how can I be upset?

There was the previous project with Ives, which you guys abandoned because of something similar—

That was a new idea, and then Pixar came out with something even more similar: *Inside Out*. The segregation of personality. It was an idea I'd had for twenty years, and Pixar did it and I didn't, because I delayed too long. But they had one idea I didn't have.

What was the idea that they had that you didn't?

That sadness is the necessary part.

And what was yours?

My idea is that every moment of human intercourse—like right now, between you and me—there are sixty-four of you in this room and sixty-four of me in this room that we bring into a conversation. So every sentence we say, any intercourse we have, is so filled with layers, and I personalized those by having two people meet in an airport. Their planes are delayed, and they start chatting. They have those vouchers for an overnight stay, so he's flirting with her, and he says, "Why don't you come up to the room for a drink?" And suddenly the entire stage goes berserk, and we're in the middle of a party, and there are twelve people, and now we play the exact same scene over again—but this time a lot is going on. But the first fifteen minutes were just talk. And they drink, and they get a little drunker. And then we play it all over again. Each person has a chorus, and at the very end your chorus gets together, and my chorus gets together, and they consummate. And I just delayed too long. I actually wrote some stuff, and so did David—

Huh. And where do those songs now live? In the box?
"Live" is not quite the word. [*Laughs*] They're in the box, yeah.

And you would never have them played as one-offs?
No. Because the kind of stuff I write, the music and the lyrics are so intertwined.

But your songs do get played—you can go to any piano bar and hear "Not While I'm Around"—so people get many of the songs without the context of the characters.
It's not about that. It's about the actual lyric. It's not even about the context. Unless I have a need for a song called "Not While I'm Around," it doesn't matter who the characters are. Well, God knows the history of musical theater is filled with tunes that went from one place to another. But to do that, you're admitting that your well is running dry, which I think is psychologically not good. And don't think I haven't been *very* close to that edge of that well, man—*particularly* these days. But I'm not doing it if I can help it.

Do you find the music and the lyrics harder today? Or one is harder, and one is not?
Both. I just feel less inventive. And, also, I feel I've written it before. "Oh, I've used that." Also the constant feeling, which is not unreal, of being old-fashioned.

You feel that way?

Well, I am. I mean, you know, the kind of music I write has nothing to do with anything in pop music since the mid-'50s.

Well personally, I don't think genius is ever old-fashioned.

[*He makes a mock bow of mock gratitude.*] Well, thank you for the word. But my feeling—I really believe this—I think it's the supreme geniuses, like Picasso, Stravinsky, who are able to take in the changes in their world and incorporate them into their own work. You know, Stravinsky took atonal music and wrote things like *Agon* and then decided, "Eh, I don't like it so much." But he was able to incorporate it. Picasso just took every style that was going on, and it was always Picasso, but he sucked in everything in the artistic air. And I feel very strongly about that. And I think if Gershwin were alive he'd find a way of using, you know, rock and pop and rap and all that, because he was alive to everything going on around him, and he sucked it in. [*He makes a sucking noise.*]

And you don't find you do that?

No. Because pop music and rock music with rare exceptions it doesn't make me want to listen a lot. For me the lifeblood of music is harmony, and that is not what pop and rock are interested in. They are interested in visceral; they are interested in rhythm; they are interested particularly in sound and orchestrations and effects. And it's not that I am not interested. It's just that that does not make me want to write. That's not what I write.

Have you ever tried to—?

A lot of pop and rock comes about because the people who write it are the people who sing and play it. I am *not* a performer. That's just not my temperament; that's not the way I was brought up. We do what we did in our childhood. We like what we like. My whole generation doesn't write pop or rock. And I think of Burt Shevelove's phrase about—I'm just debating whether—OK, I'll say it. When Burt heard Lenny Bernstein's *Mass*, which has a whole rock section: "Rip Van With-It." [*Laughs*]

So that's the fear?

Yeah. I don't want to be that. And then Jule Styne trying to put it in "Hallelujah, Baby!"—it's just embarrassing. It's not in their blood, you know? You write what's in your blood!

That's so interesting—

I just don't want to fall into that trap of writing something that doesn't come from what I want to write but what I think I ought to write. And that's the lesson any creative artist has to learn. Write what you want to write. Don't write what you think people want you to write, but what *you* want to write. Write what you want to write.

This feeling weighs on you, though.

All the time. And it holds me back, because I think I'm gonna be a fool in public. I remember making fun of Victor Herbert and Rudolf Friml with my father. There were two kinds of musicals in the '20s. There were the kick-'em-up, chorus line musicals, and the smartass ones I like like Rodgers and

Hart and Cole Porter, and then there were the operettas. My father loved operettas, and I thought, "Oh, c'mon! This old-fashioned shit!" I still think it's old-fashioned shit, but nevertheless. Now I'm old-fashioned shit!

I remember my father listening to Dave Brubeck—remember Dave Brubeck?

I knew him!

My father loved "Take Five."

"Take Five" is great.

You know, when I would sit there with him—the young are so intolerant—

You didn't like it? I'm not really a jazz fan, but "Take Five" is special—the spirit of it, the inventiveness of it.

So how do you push those doubts away when you're writing?

I don't. I mean, they're there all the time.

And presumably, when you wrote *Follies*, you had no such anxiety?

Well, that's different! There I was doing pastiche. I mean, half the score is pastiche. So what I was doing was I was enfolding them—I was hugging them. But also, in *Follies* there is only *one* operetta number, which is one of the big showstoppers, which was the first one I wrote, called "One More Kiss." But all the others were of the music I grew up with: [Jerome] Kern, Rodgers and Hart, Burton Lane, all those people. So, it's not comparable. I wasn't doing pastiche of stuff I didn't like.

Company had a very au courant feel to it.

Yeah. It had a soft-rocky feel, but only really in the opening number. Also I had a bossa nova number in it.

But also culturally. In *Company*, you brought news to people about the culture that they were currently living in.

I was just writing about the generation of people I knew. Actually, I was really writing about the people George Furth knew. He was pretty close to my age, but he came from a whole other culture, California culture. I came from, you know, New York upper-middle-class culture. And those combined. But the attitude of *Company* is very much George, because it's all built on his little plays . . . The springboard and the viewpoint and the tone and flavor of *Company* are all George Furth, and I'm imitating George Furth. That's what I do best: imitate the playwright.

So there is always a book for you before you even begin writing the songs?

Not necessarily. In the case of George, yes, there were these little playlets. But in all the other cases, or almost all of them, it's sitting with a book writer, and then the book writer writes a scene or two, and I get the flavor of the dialogue and the flavor of the characters. We discuss them—I know who they are—but until your version of that character and his version of that character are the same character, it could be quite different in tone, because you're different writers. So I wait, and I do what an actor does: I get into the character. By the time I get through, I know the character better than the author does, because I've looked at every sentence the author has written and quite often questioned them. Why does she say, "blue bottle" there rather than "green canister."

And in the case of the Buñuel—

We are making up our own characters based on the Buñuel characters. But the thing is, Buñuel doesn't have characters, and he doesn't have plot, which is why we are having difficulty. But David Ives is creating characters based on those. I mean, we have talked about the characters at great length between us, but he's the one who sits down and writes the sentences that I then start to play with . . . we have huge long discussions with the book writer over many weeks, because the worst mistake you can make, in a collaboration, is writing different musicals. You think you're writing the same one but you're not, because it's very deceptive.

What's the closest that's ever come to happening?

Oh, gosh. It isn't that it came close. It was difficult for me in *Sunday in the Park with George* that I think the poetry is in what [Lapine] was writing. Oh, another one was *Gypsy*. I said to Arthur [Laurents], after he had written a few scenes, "I don't see this as a musical—I just think this is so good." And he said, "Oh no, Steve. If I were writing this as a play, it wouldn't be half so broad, the strokes that I am making. I mean, I know what a musical is, and there isn't much time to develop the characters and dialogue." He said it would be an entirely different thing. And I understood what he meant.

Oh yes, I am sorry! I am leaving out the big example! *A Funny Thing Happened on the Way to the Forum*. We wrote it, and then I decided to show it to Jim Goldman, the one who wrote *Follies*. He was just somebody I knew and respected, and we were friends. So I gave it to him and played it for him. He said, "I think the book is really wonderful. The score is really elegant." And I said, "Oh, that's good." I said to him that I had this awful feeling in my stomach. I said that I guessed I was just being neurotic, and he said, "No, it's not neurotic. There's a real problem. The book and score don't go together. Burt and Larry have written a very high-class low comedy, and you have written an elegant salon score, and they have nothing to do with each other." These are not exact quotes, but the essence, and he was right. And we got out-of-town and the show was in trouble and part of it was exactly what he talked about.

What was the solution?

The solution was getting Jerry Robbins in. I had written two opening numbers—I wrote one number that was probably just right for the score, but [the director] George Abbott said that he couldn't hum it. So that was the end of that. [*Sighs*] And so then I wrote another song called "Love Is in the Air," which was lighthearted, elegant, I don't mean elegant like Noël Coward. I mean airy, and filled with little puns, and chock with charm—and the show was a disaster. So Jerry Robbins came down at my behest, and said, "You gotta write a number for the opening. The audience thinks they're going to be in for a lighthearted, light comedy, instead of which it's a baggy-pants musical. You gotta write one with baggy pants." And I played the first one for him, and he said, "That's the right one!" And I said, "Well, George won't have it." And he said, "Then, Steve, write another one!" Doesn't matter if you're right or wrong.

That's a very important lesson in showbiz. Many a show

has tripped over the fact that people hate to be wrong. One of the things I've learned in analysis is that there's nothing wrong with being wrong. A lot of people—and I'm sure you've worked with them—think it's a shameful thing to be wrong. Anyway, I *wanted* Jerry to say, "You're right, George Abbott is wrong, I'm going to tell him." All he said was, "Write another one, Steve—and don't write any jokes. I'll do the jokes. Just write an opening number that says, folks, you're gonna watch a baggy-pants show, and I'll stage it, and I'll do the jokes. No jokes, Steve!" And, boy, was he right. It made the show a hit overnight.

But there are jokes in it. The lyrics are hilarious!

No, they are not. If you think about it, they are not. "Comedy Tonight"?

[I (unwisely) sing but I suppose he is hardened to this sort of thing.] "Weighty affairs will just have to wait."

Puns! Those are called puns! But that is not a joke. That is not Jerry's point. That tells the audience, "Oh, you're in for a pun evening!" For those of them who love language, then it will be a delight.

So what would a joke be like?

It's Zero Mostel with a third leg! You didn't see the opening, the way we staged it. It's probably the best opening number we have ever staged. At the end of that number, we could have drawn the curtain down, the audience would have been happy, they would have never asked for their money back. And they would have recommended it to their friends! It was just about the best six minutes, seven minutes of showbiz you have ever seen. Screamingly funny. All having to do with what Jerry did.

Is it on tape at Lincoln Center, do you know?

No. Those were not the days when they did that. That's too early. There is a version of it on tape in this show called *Jerry Robbins' Broadway*, with Jason Alexander in the Zero Mostel part—a watered-down version of what it was originally. But oh man, the inventiveness . . . it was hilarious. Oh, gosh. It was just great!

So, when Jerry says, "Don't write any jokes," he means—

What he wanted was, he wanted wallpaper.

So what does a baggy-pants musical mean to you?

It means a farce! But not farce in the Feydeau sense. Farce in the low . . .

Burlesque?

Yes, exactly! That kind of farce. Hiding under the beds.

You wrote it quickly, right? The song that fixed the show.

Yeah, yeah. Jerry came down on Friday, and we started rehearsing on Monday.

In that era, did you feel no fear?

Oh no! I was terrified. It was my first show with music on Broadway, and I couldn't understand it. We all stood in New Haven and couldn't understand why the audience didn't like it—because it's really funny. In my opinion, the best farce ever written. I think the book is nothing short of brilliant, and it's proven to be over the years. It's always funny, and it's *beautifully* worked out in terms of plot. At any rate, I wanted the show to work. And it was clear that it wasn't working. We had a matinee at I guess a twelve-hundred-, fifteen-hundred-seat house in Washington with about fifty people in the audience. I said to Hal [Prince], "Let's invite them all back to the hotel for a drink."

That's amazing. God!

And I'll tell you another story. George Abbott, as you probably know, was known as the greatest musical doctor. He would always be called in from out of town to fix the shows. So we're all standing in the back of the theater in New Haven, George and Hal and Bobby and Burt and Larry, and the show is sinking, and George turned to us and said, "I don't know what to do! You better call in George Abbott!"

That's good!

It's true! And between us, it's the only funny thing I ever heard George Abbott say. The man had a complete lack of humor. Burt and Larry had to explain some of the jokes to him. Literally. It happened often. I have no explanation. I didn't know George that well. But I never heard him say anything funny. I never even heard him *laugh*. He was very authoritarian. He was a commanding guy.

Was he from a different background than we are?

Well, he was an actor. He was an actor for many years. And then he was a playwright, and then he was a director.

[I take a sip of my soda water.] So, returning to Byoon-well: How to create characters if there are no characters?

Talk to David!

They could be anything, no?

They are in a situation. They are slightly defined by the situation. They represent a certain aspect of society. That's why we call it *The Discreet Charm of the Bourgeoisie*. These are our own versions. These are the American versions of the French bourgeoisie—you know, the movers, moneyed people, people in power. Power is too big a word, but people who move society. The social animals. The well-off. The equivalent of the beau monde people. We have fashioned them after certain people who are in the newspapers.

And what's the conflict?

Good question. There isn't any. That's the problem with Buñuel: there never is. They're episodic. His movies are episodic. They are what you call—in the highest sense—satire. What we're hoping to do is—it's a ship of fools. We're hoping the audience gets involved with their tribulations. And, also, unlike the Buñuel movies, it *is* funny. And that is one of the things the readings have proved. It's very funny. I should say it's funny. We'll see how "very" it is. So it's exciting. Different tone to the movie, and certainly a different tone than the opera.

Are you sorry this is what you're working on? Or do you still feel like it's the right thing?

Well, I don't know. I don't want to say, because it will come out in print, and it won't look good . . . I don't know. I can't tell how much is me, how much is the project, how much is age, and how much is general . . .

But if I happened to be here on a day after you had done something that worked for you—

I'd probably be in a different mood, yeah. I wouldn't be giddy, but I wouldn't be depressive about it.

So you're literally working on songs at the beginning of the second act now?

Yeah, I write in order. I've just finished the first song of the second act, and I'm halfway through the second song. Just plodding ahead.

When you are doing that, when you're creating, do you sit at the piano? Like in *One Hundred and One Dalmatians*.

I try to write away from the piano, because when you're at the piano you get limited by your own technique—not to mention muscle memory. Your fingers fall in the same patterns that they've fallen into before, then you're writing the same chord progression, and the same accompaniment figures, all the things you want to be fresh about are in your muscle memory. And then there's the limited technique. And I have a very fleet right hand, and a lox left hand. So I try to write away from the piano, on music paper, think music, and then go to the piano and check it. And quite often I'll say, "Oh, that was not what I was thinking of," and I'll fiddle at the piano. But I try—it doesn't always work—but I try to write away from the piano.

*[I ask again my favorite question: whether the lyrics or the music
come first and Sondheim says it varies.]*

If you're trying to establish a musical mood, I'll go and
noodle at the piano, just noodle, and sometimes come up
with something in the way of figure or a harmonic progression that seems like it's the right *feeling*. If I know what the
song is going to be—quite often it will start with either a
title—meaning a refrain line—or an idea that can be com-
pressed into a few words, but they tend to come together at
the same time. Or often I will write a lyric and write notes
at the same time, without knowing exactly what the notes
are, but knowing that this note is going to be higher over
this word, and this word will have a higher note than that
word: this one is going to be "ba-dum-bum," and this one is
going to be "bum-ba-dum-dum," or whatever. I write little
notations, the melodic rhythms.

That's very useful, to know what the rhythm is going to
be, because that helps propel the contours of the melody. And
that is another thing: because I write very conversational
lyrics—I mean, that's what I *like* to do, that's what I'm
trained to do—inflection is what makes the music. In-
FLEC-tion. That word is going to be "ba-*dum*-bum." It's
not a "ba-dum-*bum*." So the inflection will dictate the contours and the rhythm of the tune and sometimes I'll go on
and fill out the actual notes and sometimes the notes will
come into my head and I'll jot them down and check them
at the piano.

And do you hear, in your head, a B-flat as a B-flat?

No. I hear the notes relative to each other. If I hear this note, and then that note, I know this one is a third below that one. That's another thing, too, at the piano. When I write at the piano, I try to write in a key I haven't written in in a long while. Because, if you're writing in B-flat all the time, you'll write the sa-a-a-me progressions.

And that's what you were trying to do this morning?

I was trying to make a modulation into something. I was writing in A Major, which I haven't written in in a *long* time. And then I had an idea for how that all could relate the whole thing to F minor and that's when I decided to go sleep . . . [*We laugh.*]

It's been so long since I studied solfège I can't remember what the flats are for A Major—

A major is three sharps.

And F Minor is?

F Minor is four flats, it's the relative minor of A-flat Major. What I am essentially doing is going from A major to A-flat, which is a halftone away, which is an odd progression, ordinarily the kind of thing you don't do, but there is a relationship between them, because A major contains G-sharp and E. And if you change the E to an F, suddenly, guess what? You have A-flat and F. So with a half-step change in the melody or, in this case, in an inner voice, you have gone from China to England—you've gone really far away, from one key to another. I said, "Ooh, that's darling! That's nice!"

To put it into the language of how we actually hear music, what would be the emotional implications of that modulation?

Oh, c'mon. You don't get real emotional implications from just *a* modulation. It's a surprise.

I just didn't know you talked this way!

I talk to myself this way! I am a trained musician. I've always been interested in what Milton Babbitt called tonicization— what other people call modulation. But what he says, which is actually a little bit more accurate—he's saying, "You've gotta tonicize something new." So here you are in the tonic of A major, and now you're going to the tonic of A-flat. That's a tonicization not a modulation. It seems like an academic distinction, but it lays out the path more clearly if you think of it that way: that you're temporarily making a tonic out of a completely foreign key.

Would you use it for a surprise?

That's what it's about. What it's about is making things surprising, but inevitable. That's the great principle of all art that takes place in time. That can be even true in painting, which does not take place in time, but, you know: "Goodness gracious! What is that red spot doing in the middle of this blue painting?!"

But you have the additional, particular burden or blessing of having words that go along with it—

Yes. But you do the same thing with words.

Is there an example from one of your earlier musicals where you did something like this and are pleased?

I do little bits of this all the time. Well, "Too Many Mornings" does this, in *Follies*. When I wrote it, it began in B major, and ended in F major, which is as far away as you can get tonally. And *nobody* has ever noticed it. It sounds like it begins and ends the way all songs begin and end—in the same key. And the F, which doesn't belong in the key of B major, occurs very early on in a chord. But Milton taught me those principles of how you pair things around, so when it does land for the audience, it's both surprising and inevitable, because you lodged a little thing at the back of their heads. But, you know, that's all technique.

Technique is interesting!

Well, it is if you're interested in technique in any art. I am! Sheepshearing: I want to know exactly how you take the wool off and what do you do—do you take it down to the root? I love the details of technique—of art in particular, but also anything, any craft. I don't know how people figure out how to do things.

Mm-hmm. I'm just trying to relate this to some actual character in any of the musicals. There's technique in *Sunday in the Park with George*, in the first act, isn't there?

Well, he talks about it. As a matter of fact, when we first started to write it, James [Lapine] knew an abstract painter, a Jackson Pollock type, not drip painting but— And he said, "Let's go watch him." Because I wanted to know, in a painting like a Jackson Pollock, how does he decide whether that is going to be red or blue? We just watched this guy paint, and we looked at his canvas, which looked to me like somebody had splattered a lot of paint on it. And I thought, "What made him do that?" But the point is, any art is a matter of a hundred thousand little decisions you make. And that's called technique: the principle behind the decisions.

Do you do other things? Like, do you cook? You don't garden, obviously.

It's funny you say about cooking, 'cause if I'd come from a family where there was cooking, I think I might've been— what I love about cooking is, I read recipes. I don't mean religiously, but every now and then in the *New York Times*, I'll read a recipe. And even though I don't understand half the terms, like the difference between satay and sauté or whatever, I *love* the thing of, "Now bring it to a simmer, simmer for three minutes, and then immediately douse it in the cold water." Or whatever it might be. So, I *would* have become a cook, but otherwise—I have no other skills.

There are no hobbies?

Nah, nah.

There's games!

Well, I used to make crossword puzzles.

You made them?

Oh yeah! A book of them. You know, I did puzzles for *New York* magazine when it first started. The first issue. Gloria Steinem was a friend, and she was a friend of Clay Felker. And Clay said, "You want to do puzzles?" And I said, "Well,

I will, but if I do crossword puzzles, I'm going to do the kind that nobody knows around here—they're called cryptic puzzles." And the only cryptic puzzle that had ever been printed in the United States was in *The Nation*. A guy named Frank Lewis did it based on, or similar to, the London *Times* crossword puzzle. Then there were the Puns and Anagrams in the *New York Times*—every third week there was a Puns and Anagrams when I was in my teens. But otherwise, there had never been any cryptic puzzles, and I'd been doing cryptic puzzles from two publications in London: one called *The Listener* and the other, the *Sunday Observer*. And in fact, there were competitions I used to enter.

Did you ever win?

No, but I got honorable mention a few times. They were done by a man named Ximenes.

Do you ever try to do the *New Yorker* cartoon on the back page?

Yeah, just for fun.

Do you ever come close?

Oh no, I've never sent anything in. I've just thought about it. I love that, I love that, I love that!

In a way they're kinda like lyrics, because when they're good, you can't imagine anything else being the caption.

Fresh but inevitable. That's that note—surprising, but inevitable. That's what I meant: "Where did that come from? Oh, of course! It *had* to be in B-flat!"

Right! And the other thing is, you know, you look at the names of the people, and they're from all over the world.

Of course!

[He tells the story of quitting the puzzle gig after two years, after thinking to himself, "I have to do man's work. I have to write a show."]

Do you still play games?

Not anymore. Everybody I played games with has died. [*We laugh.*]

You're in a cheery mood!

[*Laughs*] Well, it's true! I used to have game-mates, but they're all dead. They're all my generation, many of whom are dead.

So those games are just props at this point?

Well, first of all, they weren't the kinds of games—I *invented* some games, but they weren't the kinds of games that you carry into a room.

So, you never did board games?

Oh yes, I did! The first game I invented was called Stardom, when I was in California writing *Topper*. And the point of Stardom was that it was a board game where you fucked your way to the top.

So what were the—

It was a stylized map of Beverly Hills, with the homes of— let me think how many—about forty movie stars. But they were of different categories. There were the big stars like

Greta Garbo. And then there were the middle stars like, I don't know, Elizabeth Scott. And then there were starlets like Ann Rutherford. It was all women, so it was a very anti-feminist game, I guess. And you threw dice and traveled through all of these pathways, et cetera. There were four categories: extra player, starlet, featured player, and star. And you had to fuck your way up. So you got a secret invitation to sleep with an extra, which was the lowest of the categories. You got it by picking a card. Now, the idea was, you wanted to make your way to that person's house without other people knowing where you were going, 'cause if they thought they knew it, they could send an item in to Louella Parsons, and you would be exposed, and you would have to begin all over again and find another person to sleep with.

[*Laughing*] And the characters are men sleeping with these women—

It wasn't ever delineated—it was just that all the movie people were all women. And the idea was that after you got through the four categories, *then* you got an invitation to sleep with the greatest star of all, and that was Norma Desmond, who had an estate in the corner of the board.

Was there a technique? Or was it just rolling the dice?

No, just rolling the dice! And faking it, because if you could *fool* somebody into thinking you were going *there* . . .

Oh, I see.

So there were ways—there was more to it. And of course, once you got to the house of the lowest category, then you got an invitation to the next category. And then you got an invitation to the next. Anyway, that was one. Then I did one, it was really based on theater, called the Game of Hal Prince, in which you put on shows, and *Variety* came out each week and gave you the grosses. And Hal always won because it was really based on the economics of the Broadway theater, which is: How do you balance the cost of putting on the show, the possible weekly grosses if you get good reviews, what you do if you get mixed reviews—because in those days, there were seven newspapers. And so there were seven reviews, and each had a different point count. It was all very carefully worked out. And I was very pleased because Hal always won.

Why did he always win?

Because he was a producer! And he understood what the principle was—I invented the game for him.

So now, when you're not working, or thinking of working, are you daydreaming? Are you looking at the sky?

Nah. I'm . . .

So you're just literally here alone—you get the whole day. And you don't take walks?

I used to do a lot of walking around here. I have one route that's five miles long, and another route that's three miles long. But I haven't done it in a while, no.

Yeah, that would be tiring at this point. Physically, probably, walking on these hills is not very pleasant.

Well, at this age, it's a little, you know—my back, my balance, and all the depredations of age. But I used to do it all the time.

And I know you don't really watch TV.

I watch old movies.

Oh, you do?

Yeah. My idea of old movies is the 1930s. The movies of my childhood, some of which I never saw. Many of which I never saw. So, I have those. I just got as a matter of fact, there is a lady named Jane Klain—

There's a rhyme right there!

And she works for the Museum of Television and Radio [now the Paley Center for Media], and she is great at tracking down lost tapes. And what she tracked down was Shirley Booth in *The Glass Menagerie*, which had been lost for years and years and years. And she managed to reassemble it, and I started watching that last night.

She did that just for you?

No, no. But she told me, 'cause she knows my taste, and she said, "I thought you might be interested," and I said, "I sure would be."

So—how do you divide up your day when you have a whole day?

I try to work. And if not—I am a very slow reader, so it takes me a long time to read the *Times*.

Do you read the whole thing?

I read the news. I'm always interested in international news and New York City news. I read the arts section. And I read the obits, which I never used to do, because I want to see what everyone died of. [*Laughs*] I don't read sports. I look at the headlines of the business, to see if there is anything in there that interests me.

Do you think about death a lot?
Mm-hmm, all the time.

What do you think about it?

[*He speaks slowly, almost in a ghostly voice.*]

I think it's a bourne from which no traveler returns.

Do you have a way of conceptualizing it?
No, no. It's the usual thing. I don't mind dying. I just hate—I just don't want it to be uncomfortable. And I don't want it to be prolonged.

So you fear losing your skills more than—
Yes. That and pain. So many deaths are so unpleasant. *Dying* is so unpleasant. But I do think about it.

And do you worry about not finishing this work because—
No.

Are there other ideas waiting in the wings for you?
No, no. I rarely have something in the future, unless it is an obligation like *Company* or something like that. I'm usually dragged into work. Occasionally, I've had my own ideas.

Which ones are your own?

Sweeney was one. *Passion* was one. Together [with Lapine], *Sunday in the Park* was one. When we finally got the idea, we were both eager to write it. And *Company* was also one.

That was your idea, but—

It was Hal's suggestion to make it a musical. George had written these plays; he had never written before. There was an actual reading in New York with John McMartin, Ron Leibman, and, I think, Kim Stanley. And George said, "The producers aren't moving." I said, "Well, my friend Hal Prince will know what to do." So I sent him to Hal, and Hal said, "You know what I think? I think they should be made into a musical." So he was the producer, and he got George in from California. We sat and we talked and made it into a musical. Oh, and *Follies*, again, was something Jim Goldman and I cooked up.

But *Sweeney*, if I'm hearing right—is it fair to say that was the most purely you?

Well, I had to persuade people, that's all. Hugh [Wheeler, the book writer] didn't require much persuasion. Hal did. He said, "I hate shows with stovepipe hats." He only wanted to do big productions, 'cause he liked to show off his skills. I wanted it to be intimate and scary. But I wanted Hal, so I thought, "It can always be done small, and if Hal wants to do it big, then let's do it big and see if it works."

Is the book by you?

Oh no. Hugh Wheeler. I started to write it. I got up to page six of, like, thirty-five, and it was already an hour long. I thought, "Wait a minute. Waaaait a minute! We can't have a six-hour musical here!" So, I called Hugh Wheeler. Because we'd had a good time on *A Little Night Music*. And he was British, so he knew the legend of Sweeney Todd, and he also was the son of a bankruptcy, whatever, judge, so he knew something about the class system. So we started to write it together.

But you had created the characters at that point?

Well, no, no. It was based on a play by Christopher Bond that I went and saw at Stratford East. He had written like over a weekend, because he'd been an actor, and he was traveling with a troupe in the Midlands, and they were supposed to do a Christmas show, and someone said, "Let's do *Sweeney Todd*." So he got *Sweeney Todd*, and realized it was completely unplayable. It was this old, you know, nineteenth-century, [*mimes villainous laughter*] hee-hee-hee. So he wrote it himself, with a smashing part for himself—Tobias. And that came to Stratford East, and that's what I saw. I got out *all* the versions—there were four public versions, and Bond's was the only one that was viable. And that is the one I saw. So, it was really his. *He* created the characters. He based them partly on the Jacobean tragedy, *The Revenger's Tragedy*. And also on *The Count of Monte Cristo*.

Right, of course. What's the first song you wrote for that? Did you begin at the beginning?

Yeah, the very beginning.

My son used to go around singing part of the opening. It's got the word "shit" in it, you know.

I deliberately did that. I always wanted to be the first person to use a four-letter word on the musical stage. That's why [in *West Side Story*] I wrote, "Gee, Officer Krupke, fuck you!" And one of the coproducers practically fainted when she heard me play it.

Oh, it originally had "fuck you" in it?

Yeah. So I had to change it.

You'll be pleased to know that my kids sing it with "fuck you."

Well, they're right! So I am deprived of that. By the time of *Sweeney Todd*, of course, *Hair* had been around, and all these other shows that used four-letter words.

Did you like *Hair*, by the way?

Like? No—well, it interested me. I saw it both downtown and uptown. But that kind of music was not my kind of music. I liked what it was doing, but the music was not for me.

You mean because it's not—

Because again, it's rock. It's not my language. It's a whole other language.

I thought it was because the characters don't really exist as characters.

Oh no, they don't. It's not about characters. It's a rock concert. But you know, I loved the daringness of it.

Is it musically interesting to you?

Not to me.

I forget who wrote it.

Galt MacDermot. A Canadian.

And what came after that for him?

Their next one was called *Dude* and was a very expensive disaster. And then he wrote *Two Gentlemen of Verona*. The one with John Guare. The one that won the Tony. That's 1971.

Huh! That seems so different.

Well, it is but it isn't really. It's again essentially pop rock.

What about Andrew Lloyd Webber? Just while we're on the subject of pop rock.

What about him?

I don't know. Is there anything there for you? Do you go? Do you watch them?

Well, I've seen some. Hal directed *Phantom*, you know. I saw that. I didn't see *Sunset*, but I heard *Sunset Boulevard*. I don't remember which ones I have seen.

Is there something you take away from them, or is it just—

What do you take away from a musical? What do you mean?

I don't know. They made a lot of money.

I didn't take any of the money.

You know what I mean. Is there a thing that you learn from them?

No, no. I don't think I've really learned, really *learned* from any musicals.

Rodgers and Hammerstein?

Whoa. That's way, way, way, way back. When I was thirteen, yes, I learned something.

[This bit of conversation seems at an end. I notice behind him some workmen in a field.]

Somebody dragged some of your branches away, I assume it's hired—

[Laughs] Yes. There's a firm that comes around whenever stuff falls, and it's called Total Landscape. They come and they total your landscape.

[Laughs] That's your joke, not their joke?

That's my joke.

[Sondheim has been ruminating on the previous question.]

Anyway, no. I don't learn from musicals. Well, I'm trying to think—

I'm more fishing like, you know. if when you saw it, did you go "oy va voy" or—

No. I don't do that. That's not what I do.

[I suggest at this point that we wrap up and he give me a tour. He's just given me the possible end to my profile. It's the workmen carrying the branches away after the mention of death—and with Sondheim getting the last laugh. We are both clumsy after sitting for so long and nearly bump into each other extracting ourselves from our chairs.]

I'll go after you.

You go that way.

I'll go the other way.

[Now he takes me to a part of the house with a fireplace that is full of collectibles. It's the part of Roxbury that most resembles the Turtle Bay townhouse.]

These are just books that interest me because they're good-looking—they're wonderful to look at. [*One is a picture book about Addie and Willie.*] . . . This is a photo that was taken by Dick Avedon and made into a jigsaw puzzle by him, as a present for me. [*It is a cocksure young Sondheim in shirt and tie, hand thrust in pocket.*]

That's perfect, because it's your interest in puzzles combined with—

Exactly right.

[We pass a foot-tall theater stage with exultant bloodied figurines of Sweeney and Mrs. Lovett a friend made for him.]

Is this the room where you work?

No, no, no. I'll show you the room where I work. That's a room that has a computer in it, which I don't use very much.

But that's where my fax machine is, and that's where I store all my records. But they're all classical—they're not my stuff.

That is [Brahms's] second concerto . . . the second is maybe my favorite piece of classical music. And these small jigsaws are presents for opening night, or some were sent to me occasionally as gifts.

[We continue the tour. Glass harmonicas. Picture cabinets. We stop at his collection of transformation decks, playing cards where the pips have been transformed into works of art.]

Look at the elegance, look at the imagination, the inventiveness of these pictures.

Oh, there's the orb you were talking about, in the corner there!
Yeah, that's the orrery. And this is another one.

Oh, wow.
They move. They revolve.

Are those your Grammys up there?
A couple of them, yeah. I'm going to take them down. I want to put pictures up there. I can't stand them.

It's not very you.
No, no. It's not at all. *[He points out the window.]* That little pool house there—which is actually an extra little place to sleep, there's a bed there—I'm going to put all that stuff down there. That's going to have, what shall I say, stuff related to shows.

Did you not go to the Oscars?

Oh no. Want to hear the story? It's funny. Warren [Beatty] wanted me to go out. And about three weeks before the show, I broke my ankle, here in the country. This is a true story. Disney said, "We are so terribly sorry you can't come out, but here—please accept this as a gift." And they sent me a chocolate Oscar, with its leg broken. Which they did not intend. It happened in the shipment. How about them potatoes?

Whoa! [*Both laughing*] Oh, so you couldn't go because you couldn't go up the stairs—it wasn't because you assumed you wouldn't win or anything?

No, no, no! I thought, "Supposing I win, how am I going to get up the stairs in a cast?" So I watched from here. I was *very* surprised.

So, the workroom!

If it's not too painful—

No, not at all. It's only painful when you leave.

[*Laughing*] That's a good line!

This is all my scores and things like that. These shelves had videotapes in them, and I cleaned them out. I'm changing all my videotapes to DVDs. So, this is where I work.

[He takes me into the room dominated by a big black piano. There are posters from shows and blank music paper. I see some handwritten lyrics with the tight rhyme scheme I by now know Sondheim insists on.]

Marianne: *I like things that shine*
                          about me.
                          I like things that glow.
Would you like to dance, miss?

[Soldier putting arm around Marianne's waist.]

Marianne: *Why can I not be free?*
                          Why do I like what I see?
                          And not what I know?

[Next to these lyrics is a sheet of music paper in a key with four flats, a series of half notes and quarter notes, and the lyrics "Life in this room, in this gor-geous God-damn room." The hyphens have been stuck in to line up the syllables with the rhythm of the song. I can hear it in my head, and it sounds as special as everything that Sondheim does to my ears. But of course it's just a half-finished verse. I don't comment directly on the song at first.]

Oh, wow. What a beautiful room.

It's great, yeah! Let's see . . .

So, you'll sit there, and then if you want to be at the piano, you'll come up, and then . . .

Exactly right. I lie down to work, and you can see the yellow pad—[*He slams his hands on the piano, and it makes a ferocious sound.*]

Oh, that's dangerous—you bring the newspaper with you. When I'm writing, I'm like, whatever you do, keep all the shit away. I think it was the writer Tom McGuane who said, Go to a room, and whatever else, no magazines, if you're brave enough to . . .

Well, I'm not brave enough, which is one of the reasons why I'm so far behind.

No, no. All these different pens and pencils...

That cabinet is also from Burt. It's got all kinds of secret compartments in it for ships' papers, which I love. And this is, believe it or not, a Bagatelle game table.

And the music here—this is actually your draft?

Yeah. What happens is, I write them out in pencil, like so. Then it goes to the copyist . . . This is what I was working on—this harmonic transition.

Oh, it is thrilling to see this. It's all so abstract till you—

It is, yeah! Until you hear it. So I am filling out the melodic line. I don't always do this, but because I think I know where I'm going, I'm doing that. And I follow it with the harmony. I'm just sketching in the harmony now.

And this is the first song of the second act of the Buñuel?

Act II, Scene 1. That's the way that happens.

What in this room inspires you?

The pillows! [*Laughs*] Nothing, nothing. Just the room itself is terrific. The problem is that it's distracting, because you look out—see, the great thing in New York is that there's nothing to look at. Lenny Bernstein had a twelve-room apartment, and he wrote in a room about twice the size of this. Looked out at an alley. It had no light. It had some homemade bookshelves—not even good ones. A bar. A coffee table. A couch. An easy chair, and a piano. And that was it. No distractions . . . That is the only thing I regret: that this is so pleasant.

Alright, I'll let you get back to your torments, and I'll go to see where Twain made his last mistakes.

[*Laughs*]

It's touching, though. He just thought it was going to end differently than it ended.

I guess we all do.

I credited the quiet of the country and the absence of an entourage for the more intimate tone of our conversation. Brassy was the city; pensive was what the country was for. Most of all, I wanted to see the Buñuel finished and hear it, but at the same time I knew that in general failure breeds better conversations than success, and failure after success the best of all. I suppose in this case what I really wanted, though, was success after failure after success—we all were complicit, because a success was how this story should end. He *had* to triumph! What a burden Sondheim labored under, to have so many of us depending on him.

But was *Passion*, which had premiered on Broadway more than twenty years before, to be his last important work? It had to be acknowledged as a possibility. When Sondheim had taken me into his workroom, I had immediately imagined having again my Sondheim experience, the one I'd first had as a fifteen-year-old: a moment of complex pleasure when the music wakes and tickles and outwits your sluggish

brain while the rhymes click like castanets. I could not believe this might not be in my future. We said goodbye and
I drove on to see where Mark Twain's last house had been.
One of his children had died in the bathtub there, and the
house itself had long since burned down—a place for him of
despair and disillusion. Afterward, I went to the local library
and looked at his book collection.

CLOSING NIGHT

MARCH 2019

"I don't want to be watched."

I left things where they were for the moment—with Buñuel offtrack, there was no reason to push Sondheim. On the contrary, it seemed that doing that would be mean-spirited. But two weeks later, as fall began, I got an email from him that seemed to urge me to speed things up. "I haven't heard from you for a while, and life is getting busy—have you broken off our engagement?"

When I wrote him the same day to say of course we were still on, and to ask if he was back in town for the fall, I challenged him to find a rhyme for "rentrée." He responded with a good if obscure pun: "You refer to 'Rentrée County,' I assume." We set a time a week later, at his townhouse. I mentioned that I'd found a slant rhyme in *Bounce*, where

"Michigan" is rhymed with "rich again." I put a smiley emoticon after my discovery to show it was all in fun. He wrote me back an hour later: "The rhyme is sung by a dying man with slurred speech in a state of dementia. That's the joke. Lower your eyebrow and pay attention." Clearly, I'd irritated him—it was the closest I'd ever come to criticizing his craft, and *Bounce* was likely a sore subject. At least we had an appointment set.

I was expecting progress on the Buñuel. Why else would he want to see me so soon? The slough had been exited again. The producers were waiting at the door, and he was furnishing them with unforgettable tunes. Readings, workshops, rehearsals, previews, and then opening night! And great stories to recount about the whole experience. He wrote me soon after to reschedule, because he had to get some music ready. Was it *Company* rewrites, I asked, or Buñueliana? Buñueliana, he answered; *Company* began in November. I was glad to hear it.

I drove into the city for my visit in early October. I had by now found a good parking place to wait at as I always got to Turtle Bay early to avoid the rush-hour traffic. I called Sondheim's home to say I was there, but one of his staff told me he wasn't yet back from Connecticut. They'd call when he got home. I sat in my car, fiddling on my phone as the hours passed. I didn't know what to think. Had that strange request to hurry up and see him again been some sort of covert signal he wanted to break up? There were signs, of course—reticences, reschedulings—but wasn't that the relationship?

Eventually, I gave up and drove home. Before I could brood further, an email came from him apologizing, blaming a three-car accident on the Bronx River Parkway that resulted in a two-hour delay. And a Yankee game to back things up further! He couldn't do the next day—he'd be working with Tony Kushner on the new adaptation of *West Side Story*, to be directed by Steven Spielberg—but the week after was fine.

I said no problem, and when he didn't write back to several emails to confirm, I wrote him again, asking if I was in his spam filter. "Can't get 'Every Day a Little Death' out of my head. What is this a symptom of?" I added. Was I joking? Or did I think our Connecticut conversation had maybe gone too deep?

At last the shoe dropped. Sondheim wrote me the next day to say he had had second thoughts and wanted to call off the profile. It wasn't me, he emphasized—he'd recently sat for an interview with Lin-Manuel Miranda for the *New York Times*'s *T Magazine*. The attention paid to it served as a kind of warning about how little he liked publicity: "I've been, to use a phrase I've never used except in mockery, the cynosure of all eyes. And to use another phrase I've never used because I feel too old to do so, it's bummed me out. I'd forgotten how much I hate being in the spotlight, which is one reason I became a writer instead of, as I was urged to be at age fifteen, a concert pianist. (I wasn't good enough, anyway.)" He hoped I would forgive him and we would meet again under other circumstances.

The note, of course, upset me—my cheeks flushed with

free-floating shame—but it didn't shock me. Had this happened nine months before, when I had started the pursuit, I
might have been truly astonished. By now, however, I could
almost have foreseen it, the way, after someone breaks up
with you, you usually realize, if you were completely hon-
est with yourself, you knew it was coming all along. Sondheim was never going to go the distance. Ambivalence was as
prominent a part of his character as of the characters he created. In retrospect, the email asking where I'd gone I now saw
was obviously expressing the hope that I was going to ditch
him and spare him the (quickly passing) guilt of ditching me.

A deeper upset sank in after the first moments of humilia-
tion followed by the peculiar power rationalization can give
to ease the sting of other people's actions. My interviews had
all been slowly closing in on the connection between Sondheim the person and the artist. Sketching in that link as best
one could was the real goal after all in any effort like mine.
Sondheim had so far as I knew always frustrated such initia-
tives and now it was clear he was going to frustrate mine too.

After letting everything stew for a few days, I decided
that I wasn't just going to give up. One thing I had learned
from my experience over our two years was that even when
the door was closed, it wasn't necessarily shut for good.
And the relationship was, as they say, worth fighting for.
Sondheim was just too fascinating, too absorbing, and too
unusual for me to let go of. He was not just anyone. He was
one of the greats. And we had come so far. I would continue,
if he would.

Sondheim depended on reference books, so why shouldn't

I? I grabbed a thesaurus now and tried to match the energy of an old showstopping song in pleading for a reunion, something worthy of *Passion*, throwing in "ask," "request," "entreat," "plead," "implore," "beseech" and "prostrate-myself-on-the-floor-before-you-with-widow-level-grief." (He'd said he loved Puccini, hadn't he?) I referenced the "bourne" we would both one day go to and how he should consider what memorial he would want to leave behind in print when he was gone. I finished, "Why don't we take a breather, let the (very) tiny circus leave town, and rediscuss?"

Sondheim didn't respond to my supplication—the heroine's heartfelt aria—but when I wrote him again a few weeks later, we were back on teasing terms. I was in Rome on vacation with my family and told him a funny thing had happened when I was at the Forum. In February, three months after that, I took my kids to see the show itself at a theater in Islip on Long Island, and wrote to tell him there had been a "good house." I asked if it was time to begin again. "My pen is getting mossy," I wrote.

He said he was glad I had seen the show but was still too busy with deadlines and had had a medical scare. I pushed, but I was now to learn what I might have intuited from my first dismissal in early 2017: pushing with Sondheim got you the opposite reaction. He wrote me now that he had had time to think about my Connecticut visit and something I'd said there had made him uneasy. It was when I had asked him what he'd learned from Andrew Lloyd Webber. I didn't even remember the exchange, but now that he highlighted it, I could recall something effortful in his response.

Why had I wanted to know his opinion of Webber? he demanded now. Was I looking, he suggested, for "a marketable response"? I took this to mean something incendiary for my article to stir up some excitement. I responded, sincerely, I think, that I would have been most excited if he had said that he admired something from Webber, my example being perhaps the way Webber resolved "a diminished eighth." This assuaged nothing, of course. I had, I think, stepped off one mine onto another: Sondheim was unique, not in conversation with other contemporary musical talents. If I hadn't figured that out by now, well, as he had written before, lower your eyebrow and pay attention. He mentioned that he'd had trouble with the question from past interviewers too. "I don't entirely doubt your good intentions," Sondheim concluded, "but once bitten etc. etc. etc."

Of course, all this was standard. Profiles are fraught efforts, profiles of the famous famously fraught. But I was still upset. I had worked hard—I thought he had worked hard too—to get to a certain place of understanding, and now Sondheim was acting as if I was someone he hardly knew. I had never tried to be his friend, but I had tried to be his ideal conversational partner. It made me wonder again if I understood even in the most elementary way what it was like to be him. Hadn't he told me at the PEN benefit that people began to want to meet him "as soon as he got known," which might be either *West Side Story* or *Gypsy* or *Forum*, depending on who did the knowing. And these were, what, about sixty years before? Add to that a childhood that would have destroyed the trust of any young person, and what was I thinking? When I stopped to consider it, had I ever read a real profile of the man, one where you, say, saw him having his morning coffee or putting some tulip bulbs in the ground or shopping for a T-shirt to add to his collection? Those were the sorts of profiles I always wanted to read, because it was what's offstage for me that was real, not what was onstage. Maybe in the end I was the wrong writer for the job then.

I was beginning to accept that things were at an end—two objections were a lot, even if, to my eyes, they weren't particularly fair ones. I'm not sure why—maybe just because it had burrowed into my head almost fifty years ago, but I now upbraided him in an email with one of his best-known lyrics: "You were in love, or so you said." Look at the next line, he wrote me back within an hour: "'You should know better.' And I did." [*Cue sound of door slamming.*]

Bizarrely, though, if the article was off, the relationship was not. It was now less purposeful but not less affable, as if we were, say, friends who had once worked in an office together but now lived in different cities. Two weeks after my dismissal, for instance, I wrote him that my daughter, then twelve, had been cast as Big Deal in a production of *West Side Story* at her grade school. I mentioned she'd been given some lines originally belonging to other minor characters. He pretended outrage: "Extra lines? I'm notifying Arthur [Laurents]'s agent (who's a prick)."

I also told him I was going to see the revival of *My Fair Lady*, with its new feminist ending. He responded he hadn't heard anything positive about the show but by now it was too late to warn me. I enjoyed the production but didn't tell him. I sent a picture of the cast of my daughter's school's *West Side Story*. He loved it, saying that seeing such a young cast made him "hopeful."

Under the right circumstances, Sondheim even proved willing to get together in person. A production of *Merrily We Roll Along* opened in February 2019 at an off-Broadway house. *Merrily* was the musical Sondheim felt the critics had been most unfair to. He had refashioned it several times over the years, but now, once more, it was getting a drubbing. Sondheim wanted to help his show, which I had just seen and, of course, loved. In addition, friends who were practically family to Sondheim were involved. The music director of the new production was Alex Gemignani, the thirty-nine-year-old son of Sondheim's longtime conductor, Paul, who had conducted the original *Merrily We Roll Along*, as well as eight other Sondheim shows. Paul, eighty-one, was now on Broadway, conducting a revival of *Kiss Me, Kate*. A meeting, then, might focus on the theme of legacy that I knew was central to Sondheim, with an additional dollop of aggrievement at the critics.

At this point it had been eighteen months since Sondheim had halted the profile again, but we had never stopped corresponding, and I had never stopped thinking about the key question in any profile, much as in any play or musical: what really motivates the central character—Greed? A love of fame? Anger from childhood? Confusion about sex? Fear of death? For all the time I'd spent with him, I was still very much at the beginning of that fundamental question. To say that his baroque upbringing and later fame had left Sondheim well defended—maybe even from himself—was by now obvious. But I was also now very interested in a comment he'd made a number of times (though never to me) that I had not paid much attention to before. He had said that his great regret in life was not having children. "You want to live long enough to see your children grow up," he had told the *Times* of London in 2009. "They're not puppies. The joy is not just to have them, but to watch them change and grow." A friend of his had also mentioned to me how much he'd wished he had children. It would be a yawn of a solution to a cosmic riddle but that wouldn't mean it was the wrong one. And for those fond of constructing an artist's personality from the hints left in his work, plenty of Sondheim's musicals end extolling the wisdom of the humdrum. In seeing him with the younger Gemignani, I'd be watching him with one of his grown-up nonpuppies.

So in March 2019, I drove through the tunnel one more time, slipped into my customary parking space, and went down the stairs straight into his living room, which was exactly as it had been—the bounding dogs, the games under glass, the fussy furniture, and the exits and entrances from the staircases. One thing had changed—though no one told me. Sometime recently, more than a year before, Sondheim and Romley had married. Sondheim was now a spouse!—though Romley was not there that night. Sondheim met me in a black T-shirt with the word "Golem" on it—fruit, he said, of a visit to Prague—and we sat once more and talked. The Gemignanis were our chaperones, both garrulous, big

men with energy and a huge love for Sondheim. Addie and
Willie were the entertainment.

PAUL GEMIGNANI [*Asking about the poodles*] How old are
they now?

S.S.: Fourteen and twelve.

P.G.: Wow, you are a lucky man. You are really lucky.

S.S.: [*To Addie and Willie*] Yes, I know. I love you.

ALEX GEMIGNANI: Hi pups!

S.S.: They're happy to see strangers. It's very unusual. I'm
too old now to play with them, throw a ball. If I lean over to
pick up a ball, I fall over.

[*Everyone laughs.*]

S.S.: It's true!

P.G.: Well, that could be fun, too.

S.S.: So, have you been around the campus [the Roundabout
Theatre, where *Merrily* is playing] recently?

A.G.: I have not. I'm going Saturday for both shows.

S.S.: Do you know if the morale is any good?

A.G.: Morale seems to be fine!

P.G.: **They told me that they were doing great.**

S.S.: Oh, that's good. I haven't been . . . I was mainly talking about the cast.

A.G.: **The reports are all good. The audiences have been strong.**

S.S.: Just, you know, we all know how actors feel when they get slammed against the wall, so . . .

A.G.: **Yes, yes.**

S.S.: That's good. [*To Paul Gemignani*] How's everything at *Kiss Me* . . . [*he delays the word for a beat*] *Kate*?

P.G.: **It's the same as it was twenty years ago. It's Baptist.**

[*Everyone chuckles.*]

P.G.: **It's great. You know, it's a well-written piece, so—**

S.S.: Except that one line.

What's the line?

S.S.: "It's lucky I missed her gangster sister from Chicago." I think he [Cole Porter] deliberately wrote this line, because the bad line makes everything else in the song look brilliant. Suddenly, in the middle of this very elegant lyric, there's a "joke" that belongs to George Jessel, and I thought, "He didn't really do that."

P.G.: **It always gets a laugh, too. It's surprising.**

s.s.: Oh, well, that's why he did it. It's the Woody Allen kind of laugh.

But what's the joke?

s.s.: Remember, in each of the little verses—you know, "gave a new meaning to the Leaning Tower of Pisa"—there's a joke at the end of each quatrain. "Missed her gangster sister from Chicago" is just, "Oh, c'mon, Cole!" [*Laughs*]

Hm, I never noticed that before.

s.s.: [*Speaking to me, I think*] I was going to share a quote with you. It's a quote from Dorothy Parker. She says, "To all young writers: the second-best thing you can do is to buy and read *The Elements of Style*. The best thing you can do is to shoot yourself now so that you won't have to be unhappy!"

[*Everyone laughs.*]

s.s.: I slightly misquote it, but that's the idea. Anyway, OK.

[*I take my cue and begin the interview.*]

So, you guys, just to cover your connections to *Merrily*—I know a little bit. [*To Alex, the younger Gemignani*] I know you were at the original opening night. Is that right?

A.G.: Oh, gosh, I don't know! The earliest rehearsal I ever remember going to was for *Sunday in the Park*. I remember swinging by that rehearsal—it was for someone's birthday. But no, my relationship to *Merrily* other than, like, knowing Dad had done it—

P.G.: And wearing out the recording.

[*To the father*] How did you two meet?

S.S.: *Follies* had opened, and the conductor—wait a minute, let me get this straight. The first time I met Paul, he was brought in by Michael Bennett—you can correct me on this, Paul—

P.G.: To be the drummer for *Follies*, yeah. Michael's drummer recommended me. I was a conductor, and I didn't want to go back to playing drums, but my boss, Hal Hastings, basically told me that he would fire me if I didn't take the job. So I called around the country to some of my music friends, and they all said the same thing: "What in the fuck is the matter with you?" So I went, and I've never regretted it for one second.

And what was your first impression of Steve when you first met him? In what year?

S.S.: Fall of '71.

P.G.: He's a man with a big soul. I said things to him that I wouldn't say today, in terms of music, because I didn't know any better, and he took it and didn't say, "Punk, shut up." Nothing.

What kinds of things did he tell you?

P.G.: Like, "How 'bout you change this chord to that?" That kind of stuff. If I tell a musician that story, they turn ashen. But, I mean, he is one of the kindest, most collaborative people I've ever known in my life.

A.G.: I would a thousand percent agree with that.

S.S.: I agree!

[*Everyone laughs. We are in ceremony land, familiar territory.*]

[*To Sondheim*] And what was your first impression?

S.S.: What's interesting is I didn't really get to know Paul until later. The big moment is that when *Night Music* opened, Hal Hastings was the conductor, and he died. And Hal [Prince] said, "Let's get Paul to take over."

P.G.: When I took over *Night Music,* we had a meeting. Knowing Hal as you do: "When do I have to go in?" "Tomorrow." [*Everyone laughs.*] And so I said, "I can't go that fast. Maybe four days."

[*To Sondheim*] Were you nervous to have him as the conductor?

S.S.: No, not at all. First of all, I know so little about the orchestra. I just thought, "Whatever he does is right." It's like—when you hire a lawyer, you don't say, "Why did you do that?" You assume he's good. He was hired because he was good. And also, when Paul gets in front of an orchestra—I don't know if you can print this—but as I've often described, Paul does something I've never seen a conductor do, which is he fucks the orchestra, and the result is: [*whooshing noise*]. It's remarkable! I've sat in the pit occasionally, watching Paul conduct, and I thought, "If I could play the violin, I'd play for him!" You know, he has a way of connecting with an orchestra. Now, I have not seen many conductors—and in a sense, it's what Lenny did . . . But that was certainly my impression of him professionally. And then we just became friends, I guess.

[*To Alex*] And you were into Steve's music from the beginning?

A.G.: Oh yes. Addicted. *Sweeney* is still my favorite, I think, but I actually—I don't know if you remember this, Steve, but I was taking an advanced English course—this was my junior year of high school, maybe my senior year—and you had to find a piece of American literature that you loved and write a huge paper about it. And I pitched *Sweeney Todd* to the teacher, and she said sure. And I called Steve and asked him a couple questions about the show and included it in my nice bibliography at the end: "Interview with Stephen Sondheim."

Did you get an A?

[Sondheim barks with laughter.]

A.G.: **You better believe it!**

S.S.: No, he got an A sharp.

[Everyone laughs.]

And what was the role of *Merrily* in your brain before all of this? Was it one of the albums you listened to over and over?
A.G.: **Oh, sure!** *Sweeney, Merrily*—**well, also, because of where I met** *Into the Woods*—**I was eight when it first premiered, in '87. And that was the first show I remember going into work with Dad a lot. Like, I came and saw that show** *a lot*. **I would stand next to him on the podium. At the Hirschfeld, for the giants, for Merle Louise's booming voice and the footsteps, they had this** *huge* **speaker at the back of house left, and I'd seen the show twenty-five, thirty times, so when the giant was coming, I would always run over and sit on the speaker. It was the EPCOT Center version of** *Into the Woods*, **because you could feel the vibrations!**

S.S.: Ha! Oh, that's fun! And of course *Merrily* is the show where whatever period of your life you see it in, it means something different, because that's what it's about. I've had a lot of people say, "My God! I feel so differently about it."

And I'm not talking about good or bad different—just their emotional reaction.

What was your emotional reaction to seeing *Merrily* this time?
S.S.: Oh, I loved it. Well, I love the show. I always cry at the climax of "Opening Doors," when they say, "We'll worry about it on Sunday." I identify with the show very intimately. It relates to my life. It's not *about* my life, but it relates. And gosh, you know, it just touches me. Also, I love George's writing so much. George Furth is one of the most underrated writers in the American theater.

P.G.: I agree.

S.S.: Funny and sharp and—

A.G.: Unexpected.

Is *Merrily* one of the shows you feel most close to?
S.S.: It's one, certainly. Well, partly because it's always been slapped around, and you tend to like the child who gets the least attention the most, you know? So I keep wanting people not only to like it, but to appreciate George's work. It's the Dickensian child in the corner.

P.G.: That show will never go in that space that you want it to go in. It will go in its own space—and that's what makes it great. I mean, there's so much in there. Just with one lyric, just with how a character says something to you in *Merrily*. Like, when she goes, "Charlie, why can't it be like it was?" I must have heard that a trillion times. I can't sit still. I have to look away so as not to embarrass myself. That kind of thing does not exist in other pieces. There's always some place in his work that's going to happen. It's going to go, "Hello, you're alive. Feel it." Every time.

S.S.: Oh . . . see, that's why he's a good conductor. You get it!

[*Turning to Alex now*] How did you come to want to be involved with the show?
A.G.: This production? Well, Fiasco Theater Company brought me on board—gosh, three years ago or so. One of the directors, Ben [Steinfeld] and I wrote a show together and became good friends, and Ben and Noah and Jessie are the three artistic directors, and I took a meeting with them about it.

They already wanted you to do *Merrily*?
A.G.: Yeah, *Into the Woods* was very successful, and Roundabout asked them to be a company in residence. And then I'm not sure if they brought *Merrily* to Roundabout or if Roundabout brought *Merrily* to them—

S.S.: I'll bet it was their idea, because it's about them. It's about three people who have an intricate relationship, and they make things together—

A.G.: Make shows together, yeah. And I also think it's one of the intangibles that makes this production special. *Their* personal connection to the material is very rich, which you wouldn't know unless you knew them. But I think it gives it that extra sort of depth.

S.S.: Yep. Absolutely.

A.G.: When I first got on board, it was just to music-direct the workshop, and I was instantly intoxicated with their process once I started, which was deep text conversations. And then I found

out that Steve had given permission and access to past drafts . . .
The opportunity to get inside this show and approach it from a
place as if it were brand-new for our brains was—I mean, I cannot
imagine a bigger gift that Steve gave all of us by allowing that
process to happen.

So you allowed that before he was involved?

S.S.: Oh, sure. I never saw their *Cymbeline*—I just heard
enough about it. So, when they wanted to do *Into the Woods*,
I said, "Absolutely." And then I loved what I saw, so when
they wanted to do this, I said, "Of course."

A.G.: Yeah. And then we started to pull the string of curiosity, and
kept pulling it, and that allowed us to explore lots of different
things. And as a music director and then what became arranger
and orchestrator, you were responsible for maintaining the
integrity of the music. So, my questions were always about, "How
does this music serve the thing we're in pursuit of?" I mean, Dad
can speak to this, too—there's a hefty dose of sort of uncredited
arranging, if you're a good music director, because you're in the
room collaborating with actors and the writers. So, you're going
to be like, "Hey, leave beat four of the accompaniment out,
because they're doing an acting thing." Just little things that add
up to big things, you know? Little things that add up to, "How is
the dramatic moment being realized onstage?" You have to serve
that, and you have to do that all while preserving the integrity of
the score. I love that challenge, especially in music that is so rich,
and characters and drama and comedy that is so rich.

S.S.: They both have this in common. Because one of the
great things about Paul is that he's wonderful at underscoring. I like underscoring, but he not only is good at it, he
knows how to make whatever I write as underscoring work,
or how to expand it, or how to change it. I mean, we also

consult, and we confer, but that's a gift he has. Not every musician, not every composer has that.

P.G.: That's because they don't like the movies.

[Everyone laughs.]

S.S.: That's part of it. That was one of Lenny's great gifts—his underscoring. And some people don't have it, and Paul's got it.

P.G.: The underscoring before [*singing in a falsetto voice from West Side Story*] "I have a love"—Jesus.

A.G.: Yeah, that's no joke. Anyway, after several workshops and several rehearsals, I wrote Steve, and I was like, "Are you comfortable with me orchestrating this? It seems to make sense to me because I know the actors. I know the performances so well at this point. I want to be able to tailor this stuff to specific things that we've been building for three years." And he, of course, was like, "Sure!" [*Laughing*] So it became just a natural thing. And again, this is where training as a musician comes in very, very handy—

S.S.: He plays so many instruments. One of the things about orchestrating—Jonathan Tunick said, "You cannot be a good orchestrator until you play with an orchestra." He just made that a pronouncement. I don't know what Rimsky-Korsakov would say about that—well, come to think of it, he did play with a band—but that's what's going on here.

P.G.: It just informs you the magic isn't all in the keyboard or all in the cello. You have to know what other things can bring. Like, the difference between choosing a clarinet and a violin to play a sentimental moment. If you've never played in an orchestra, you have no connection with that happening. You sit there and play all these classical composers, and *they* know, and suddenly out of no place Shostakovich plays a cello solo for four bars. You go, why did he do that?—but then, why are you crying? So you remember that kind of stuff.

Well, what do you think are the biggest changes between your father's version and your version of the show? Does your show end with "Hills of Tomorrow"?
A.G.: Yes.

And Paul, yours is with "Our Time," right?
S.S. Well, George and I changed that. George and I rewrote this show right after it opened and closed, and we worked on it. There were a couple of productions—one in the Northwest, one in Texas, and we kind of steered it until we finally got a production in Leicester, England. And we looked at it, we thought, "OK, that's it. We finally got the show we wanted." There was no introductory thing—

You mean there were no graduation speeches?
S.S.: Yeah, yeah, no, that was cut by England. What happened was, after it closed in New York—maybe you know this—Lapine decided he wanted to do it. So he got together with George and me and gave us some—what shall I say?—not instructions, but things that might help the show, which had to do with structural stuff. And then we did a production in La Jolla, and that worked very well, and that became the basis for what George and I then rewrote and got to Leicester. But it was Lapine who made the sea change from the first production to this production—that's the big moment.

P.G.: It's also one of the economic losses we have had in theater, which is if that show had gone out of town, we would have fixed it. We had no time! You know, the people are here in your face right when you come in the door, and there was no time. When we went out of town with *Follies* or any other show—and it suddenly got so expensive to do that, they stopped it. It's one of the greatest losses from a writing point of view in the musical theater world.

S.S.: Right, it became completely impractical. No matter how—if you played *capacity* in Detroit, you still lost money.

P.G.: You still lost money!

S.S.: And a *lot* of money.

A.G.: But the thing that's interesting, too, with what you're saying, Dad, is that development is the name of the game with musicals. And so, you know, if you think of something like *Hamilton*, which had nine years, ten years of people being like, "OK, do a little more. Do a little more." And every show—this is what I mean—

P.G.: This is why Michael [Bennett] did nine workshops of *Dreamgirls*. Nine! Nobody saw it but four of us for all those nine things, because it takes that long to do something.

A.G.: The most disappointing thing for me when I go see a new musical is the feeling that it didn't have enough time. Because you can see the germs of great ideas, and you can *see* the potential of the thing.

P.G.: And in a society that is instantaneous gratification all the time, you do a show like that, and it has great potential—it's gone, pal. You never see it again.

But this one came around—
P.G.: The quality of writing is different.

S.S.: You may not know this—maybe nobody knows this—but the first show that ever did a workshop of any sort, meaning the first show that did not fix itself by going out of town—up until this show that I will mention, a show always opened out of town. You worked on it out of town. If you had enough time, you got it to New York. Usually the first act was fine, the second act was not, because you never had a chance to do the second act. The show would open in New York with a great first act and a terrible second act. And the first show—this happened with Jerome Robbins—was *A Funny Thing Happened on the Way to the Forum*. We wanted Jerry to direct it, and he was doing his usual "I don't know. I don't know. I don't know." So, he said, "Steve, why don't you go get a group of actors around a table? They'll just read it, and you'll play the score, and let's see." And it opened out of town, and it was a *disaster*. Eventually, needless to say, it turned out. But the point of the story is that it started—

A.G.: You had to hear it. It's a living—

So let's go a little bit to your changes.
A.G.: I would say the significant thing would be the transitions—how we got from year to year. Steve wrote this great song, "Merrily We Roll Along," the title song, that in the original production comes back several times to demarcate, "OK, now we're going back in time, we're going back in time, we're going back in time." And for various exploratory reasons, we decided that we wanted to do something different. Part of the decision

was that we made it one act. Part of the decision was sort of, "How do we want this information parsed out, that we're going back in time?" Which took a lot of experimenting and was changing up until—the last thing we added was Frank saying the year on the rooftop. I think that came in, like, the last minutes of the final previews.

S.S.: The original show, back in 1981, we had transitions between the scenes that dealt with what happened that year. Like, there'd be the ABSCAM scandal between 19-blah-blah-blah. So, you'd have a scene, and then you'd have a little either musical or spoken moment, which would be, like, a thirty-minute sketch: "And this happened in 1964. And *this* happened, et cetera, et cetera." And it just became too unwieldy, so the show was in some trouble. We cut all those before we opened in New York, but not all of them.

A.G.: Yeah. Part of it is we don't have a chorus. We have six people, so there wasn't really a way to make a big choral gesture. We do a couple times in the show—but I think there's actually only one moment where the full company, all six people, are singing. In our version, which is the very first transition out of LA and into the—

You mean when they're at the party?
A.G.: Yeah, but it's after the party, when they sing "Merrily." The tune. They sing at the very top of the show together as a group, as sort of an invocation.

S.S.: But then "Merrily" as a tune gets dropped. I'm sorry it's not still in the show, but I understand why.

A.G.: It comes back thematically a little bit at the very end.

But much less than in the original?
  A.G.: **Oh yes, yes.**

S.S.: I wanted it to be a motor for the show.

P.G.: **A driving force.**

S.S.: To remind the audience what the show's about, which is time.

A.G.: **So that was it. Another sort of big-ish gesture is we did a new arrangement of "Now You Know," once we decided—and, of course, talked to Steve about it—but we made the event a private event versus a public event. That obviously changed the whole course of what that song needed to be.**

S.S.: Absolutely. And then, of course, the big change is incorporating the Kaufman and Hart scene [the musical is based on their 1934 play of the same name], where he's with his in-laws and the baby——That was always, for me, the key scene in the Kaufman and Hart play, because that's a scene that lets you know why Frank became the son of a bitch he did. And so the Fiasco people decided they'd like to put that scene back in. So, the problem is, of course, it has no song in it, so in a sense it's a lump. But I think it works great, because it explains——

P.G.: **It also gives Frank a soul.**

S.S.: That is *exactly* right. And that's why in the Kaufman and Hart play, it's the key scene. But we had no room for it. I don't even remember why we never even considered it in the original, but we never even considered it.

So if you could do the musical from the ground up again, would you include that scene and write a song for it?

S.S.: Absolutely. Absolutely.

What kind of song would it be?

S.S.: Oh, c'mon. I have no—C'mon!

[*P.G. laughs heartily.*]

S.S.: First of all, you have to decide: Is it going to be his song? Her song? Are the in-laws going to be in it? Is it going to be a little group? Is it going to be an argument? Is it going to be their declaration of love despite the trouble with the in-laws? Sixty-four ways you can go! It's certainly something.

Because I know you're going to have to go, can you guys try and summarize the difference between the two *Merrily*s that you each were involved in and the original?

A.G.: I can speak to my impressions of the album. I would say that that original album has more energy and vitality and youth than almost any album that exists. I mean, it's *steaming* off the thing. You hear this hunger and this drive, and this cry out—

S.S.: First of all, the average age of the cast was maybe twenty-one.

P.G.: That's right.

S.S.: *And* they knew the show was about to close.

P.G.: Right.

s.s.: And they were recording *after* the show had closed, so it was the only chance to get this so other people could hear it. When he says hunger, that's exactly what it was.

A.G.: And the band played the score that way, too, because you could *tell* they loved it. You could tell from the downbeat of the overture that the band was just, like, "Fuck yeah." They just . . .

[*To Paul*] And you're conducting it?
A.G.: Oh yeah. You can tell. Or, I could tell. [*Laughs*] And Steve could tell!

Is it a bigger orchestra than—
A.G.: Oh God, yes . . . Twenty-something?

s.s.: I would say twenty-four.

P.G.: Twenty-four.

A.G.: We have eight.

P.G.: And it was mostly a band, which is what *Merrily* should have. It had two cellos that were the only strings in it, and the rest was a band. And that's what *Merrily*—if I had anything to say about it, that's exactly what I would have done also. And it's some of Jonathan [Tunick]'s best writing.

s.s.: And Alex's reduction—no modesty, please—has the same kind of excitement in a smaller way.

P.G.: I agree, yeah.

s.s.: It's, like, *this* size firecracker as opposed to *that* size firecracker—but it's a firecracker. It's—pew! [*Blast-off noise*]

Like that. You feel it right in the beginning. And I don't think it's enthusiasm—I think it's his orchestration.

[*A.G. laughs.*]

S.S.: I mean, the enthusiasm is there, but—

P.G.: It's a funny thing, that show, I have to say. Because of its history, it started out with what he just said—we're in a recording session, and something that we really love just got shut down. So we were like, "Here—fuck you." Right? And that's the same thing—the energy that music wells up in you, and they all play that way. This band, who—I can't believe that all of them had heard it before they played this show—I just don't believe it. I don't believe people listen to that kind of music like we do. But they play—you could tell right from the first downbeat, you know, that—this assistant girl piano player plays a *ball*. You *know* where we're going, and that's not always true either.

So, I don't really care that critics criticize it. I went and I thought it was terrific. I'm just curious—is it a show that cannot win the love of critics for some reason?

P.G.: First of all, let me just say one thing. If you listen to critics, you're in the wrong business. It's not what you're doing this for ... I don't think it matters whether they ever come across— they mean nothing. Look at the business happening. It doesn't matter!

S.S.: But that's not his question. His question isn't about the value of critics. He said, will they ever—and I'd like to answer that. I don't think a critic will *ever* admit he's wrong. They screwed it back then. "Screwed" is not the right word. They panned it back then, and they ain't gonna admit that it's any good now.

P.G.: **No, they can't. They can't change.**

S.S.: The only one, curious enough, who—oh, he was not one of the original critics—is [Ben] Brantley. Brantley said, you know, "This show is still broken in some way, but gee, it's good. You know?"

[Paul has to go. There's a performance of Kiss Me, Kate *that night.]*

Is it because of Franklin Shepard? Is that why it can't win love?

S.S.: I think it's really about critics not wanting to change their views. To admit, quote, that they were wrong, end quote. Almost never does a critic say, "I was wrong." The only time I know was a critic named Howard Kissel who panned *Sunday at the Park with George* fiercely and then, on revival, said, "You know something? I think I was wrong." It's the only time I've ever known a critic to go back and say, "I was wrong." They won't do it, and that's why. So, the answer is no.

Alex, you didn't get a chance to talk about the *Merrily* that you made. How do you define it as separate from the *Merrily* that your father made?

A.G.: First of all, I just want to say, because I've actually done a lot of revivals as an actor: you can't do these things without the original productions having been so iconic, I don't think. And I think part of the gift that Steve is giving with his work again and again is the generosity of collaboration, allowing all these people, these artists, to take a look at his work again. And that's incredibly brave. If anybody who's written anything would have any right to say, "No, don't look at my shows, just do the version that was the original," Steve would have the right to do that. But he doesn't. And it's incredibly brave.

Yeah, I'm very impressed by how you leave the door open.

S.S.: Everybody says, "Oh, it's so brave!" I've said so many times, out loud and in public, the joy of the theater is that from generation to generation, from year to year, the production is alive, because it can be done differently. Even night to night, as we all know. It's not the same show tonight as it was last night. And that's so much better than writing for the movies, where it's *there*, and that may be perfect, but that's permanent. The fun is allowing people to reinterpret.

A.G.: So, yeah, I would say the intimacy of our production shines a light on the story from a different angle. And I think it focuses on the friendship in a way that I think the original focused on a broader thing.

What was the broader thing?

A.G.: Ah, success, or . . .

S.S.: Yeah. Kaufman and Hart wrote a play about the perils of success. Actually, the original title of the play was *Americana*. They were talking about what happened in America after the First World War, where suddenly money, success, and then the crash, and then money and success—and that's what they were writing about, was what happened to the sense of American values in the intervening years between 1918 and 1934. And when we started to write this thing, we weren't interested in that, because, unless you grew up in that period, we weren't talking about what happened after the First World War. Although, expedience is in it, and a number of songs—because that happened during the Reagan era. Expedience became everything. And that's in a sense what Kaufman and Hart were writing about. But then

I realized, *while* I'm writing this show, that's fundamental to include, but it's about friendship. Now, Kaufman and Hart did—if anything, that was a *minor* theme, was the friendship between these two guys. Because the friendship with the woman wasn't as crucial as it was in the musical version.

A.G.: **It wasn't the glue.**

S.S.: Yeah, and now that's *really* what it means. That's what moves me about it. And I realized that, you know, particularly—actually, I realized after Lapine's version. Lapine, his curtain moment was not the one that was done in California but it was in rehearsal, made both George and me burst into tears, because it was about the friendship between these two guys.

It ends on "Our Time"?
S.S.: Lapine's version, in the rehearsal, the graduation song came at the end, and the two of them had written it together at their school. And when the song was over—I'm gonna cry again—they started toward each other to embrace. Blackout. That's all I can tell you. Before they embraced. It was *stunning*. But then we decided to cut the graduation end, so . . .

Oh, you decided to cut that?
S.S.: Oh yeah, we cut the graduation. It made it—gosh, there are so many reasons. But, you know, opening it with the graduation, and the talk to the students, and all that. It just . . .

But you do open with the graduation.

S.S.: Yeah, but not with responses from the kids, and that sort of thing. Back then, when it opened with the graduation, they sang the *song* at the beginning, so it was a big moment. In the Kaufman and Hart, it ends with his graduation speech, which is "To thine own self be true," but it's only— it's not about making excuses, it's about the idealism of "to thine own self be true."

I can't even imagine what the play's like. I saw they were selling it at the Roundabout Theatre—

S.S.: The play? You gotta read it.

Really?

S.S.: The brilliance of the plotting of that play—Agatha Christie should turn in her grave.

It's funny, they don't—you know, when you say their names—

S.S.: Nobody knows who they are . . . The wisdom, the wit! How about when [Kaufman] [*laughing*] came and saw a play he had directed, and a week later, he brought the cast together and said, "Please take out the improvements." And I'll tell you a parenthetical. Kaufman was a big bridge player, and one day he was up at, like, the Harmonie Club or one of those places where you play with different partners. He didn't know his partner, and so at one point the partner said, "Excuse me, I have to go to the bathroom." And when he left, Kaufman said to the other two people, "For the first time this afternoon, I know what he's got in his hand."

He's just one of those guys from that period where I just, you know—

S.S.: Yeah, he and Dorothy Parker. You just can't believe
they said it. It's because the good stuff was repeated, the bad
stuff wasn't! Kaufman was somebody you didn't want to
cross, I'll tell you that. [*Laughing*]

Really?

S.S.: Not in a dark alley!

Did you overlap?

S.S.: Oh, my lifetime did, sure, because he was on that TV
show [*This Is Show Business*]—

But you didn't actually—

S.S.: Oh, I never met him.

And you didn't need permission to make the adaptation, did you?

S.S.: No, not at all. But if you want an anecdote, I'll tell it.
[*Laughs*] OK, so he wrote a play—let's get this right—when
I was in college, he had written a play with Marc Connelly
called *Beggar on Horseback*, which I loved. That was the first
musical I did. My sophomore year in college I wrote an adaptation of that, and I put the script—because I had to send
it to him, I thought, I better put the script in a binder—and
mailed it to him. And back came a letter saying, "I'm terribly
sorry, but I cannot give you permission to produce this as
your show."

Oh, shit.

S.S.: [*Beat*] He kept the binder.

Because he wanted to use it?

    S.S.: [*Laughing*] I just got the paper back!

    A.G.: [*Still laughing*] He was like, "I could use this for something!"

    S.S.: Exactly!

[A.G. excuses himself to head home to be with his family.]

OK, I appreciate your time. I really enjoyed it.

    A.G. [*To Sondheim*]: I'm gonna email you about *Saturday Night*, because I'm doing the Second Stage benefit.

    S.S.: What time is it, do you know?

    A.G.: Seven PM.

    S.S.: Whoa!

    A.G.: Well, we're being contained to eighty minutes—which means we have to make some trims.

    S.S.: Fair enough. Make it "Thursday Night!" Thanks for coming over!

[Alex Gemignani leaves.]

    S.S.: That's the first show I ever wrote: "Saturday Night." It was done at Second Stage.

That was fun! [*It's surprisingly quiet now, as if the audience has left the theater, except, of course, that I'm still here. I pause and remember that a good rhyme always gives Sondheim pleasure. He's told me so, after all. The click.*] And with Buñuel, all is well?

S.S.: [*Flatly*] No.

Talk to me.

S.S.: I'm having a lot of trouble with that stuff. That's too depressing to talk about. I mean, from a creative point of view.

Because when I saw you last, you were—

S.S.: Yeah, well I'm still—I'm a little worse, maybe.

Wow. Maybe it was just summer.

S.S.: Maybe it's summer, maybe it's Buñuel, and maybe it's age. Maybe it's a combination, but it's not summer. It's a combination of Buñuel and age.

I thought you were going to tell me they had a date and a theater and—

S.S.: No, I wouldn't.

And an actor.

S.S.: It's not about that. It's about writing.

Yeah, yeah. Anything I can do to help? [*I'm joking. I'm not joking. I don't know whether I'm joking.*]

S.S.: No, thank you.

[*Laughing*] Would you buy that rhyme? I know you've got this—

S.S.: What was the rhyme?

I just made that rhyme: Buñuel and well. I said "The Buñuel is well?"

S.S.: No, that's an identity, not a rhyme.

You're so strict! [*Saying it, I realize I've said it before to him.*]

S.S.: Well, you're asking me—that's your definition of a rhyme? You know, some people think that *phone* and *home* rhyme.

And you don't?

S.S.: I think that's an imperfect rhyme. *Buñuel* and *well* are not a rhyme. They are an *identity*. I'm just identifying these things.

Well, do you use identities in your verse?

S.S.: Oh, sometimes. The way Oscar did it is "younger than springtime am I," "gayer than laughter am I"—

Yeah, but do you do that? I can't think of an example.

S.S.: Well, I'd have to—I'm not a scholar of my work. I don't remember all of it!

I feel like you do. I feel like your memory's insane.

S.S.: My memory's good, but do you remember everything you've written? Can I quote a sentence from something you wrote five years ago, and you'd say, "Yes! I changed the word cat to dog." I'll bet not.

Two points of distinction. One: a compliment to you. Your work is at a level—

S.S.: Thank you.

Two: they're lyrics. They're more precise; they have to be much more exact.

  s.s.: Oh, you're talking about rhymes.

[*Trying one more time*] So, can we continue marching along while you're working on the Buñuel, or you just don't want to march along while you're working?

  s.s.: No, because I'm not working on the Buñuel.

Alright, but why couldn't we march along and catch up on—

  s.s.: Because I don't—

We could do early stuff—

  s.s.: No! Daniel! You must know the answer to your question. I do not want to be looked at. End of it! I don't want to be watched.

Soon I left. Sondheim was going to see Cyrille Aimée, a jazz singer "doing a series of jazz riffs on my stuff" at Birdland. The last minutes in the townhouse had been strange. First there had been Sondheim's burst of anger at the very end. It was not surprising—of course I'd known that Sondheim possessed such intensity—but still stunning to be the object of it. Afterward, the animated stage set that was Sondheim's home had suddenly felt empty and cold, and Sondheim small and lonely. That moment in the house made me worry for the one and only time about Sondheim, how old he was, how fragile, how much his life depended on an effort of will on his part that derived from his titanic talent, how repulsive failure must seem to him. Around his unique gift his world spun; absent that this house would disintegrate.

But as ever, whatever aftereffect our impasse left was too subtle for me to perceive. We were both excellent compart-mentalizers. When I called Sondheim the next day to finish the reporting for the Talk piece, our conversation was the same as ever. I asked him what he thought of Aimée's per-formance. He said he'd loved it. "She's terrific," he told me. "And I'm not even a jazz aficionado."

Sondheim liked the ensuing Talk article. Clearly, we had found our form together, the lyric of journalism, with the same delicacy and elisions. His only objection was that when he spoke of "Lenny" we didn't add his last name afterward. Surely the young had no idea who Leonard Bernstein was. "Cavils aside," he concluded, "thanks again." I asked if cavil could rhyme with Advil, and of course he wrote back, "You must be kidding!" (I had by now long since concluded that Sondheim used a rhyming dictionary not to enhance his rhyming capability but to restrict it.)

But his dismissal was fond and, led by me, our correspon-dence returned to dwelling in possibilities. The Marianne Elliott–directed *Company* with a female lead had been running in London and looked likely to transfer to New York, so I wrote him, "Is *Company* coming? I want to bake them a cake." He answered that it was too soon to know if it would find a Broadway house and to ask him in April, then July. He added that he'd seen the closing night in London and it was "thrilling." He had also checked out the return engagement of the National Theatre revival of *Follies* he had spoken of so highly to me before. He was happy to announce it contradicted Kaufman's advice on how to make a show better. In this case, the opposite had transpired: "A little recasting and a lot of small touches have made it even better," he wrote me.

The new version of *West Side Story* was filming—perhaps a new piece could be tied to that? Too late. He'd already been on the set. He might go again, but then, after Hal Prince's death in July, he was spending time with the family. I expressed my condolences. His ninetieth birthday? Any more publicity for that and he'd drown. Then COVID came. His ninetieth birthday celebration, in that lethal month of April 2020, became a Zoom fest, with Audra McDonald and Meryl Streep among those performing. I watched them all singing from their modest homes—Bernadette Peters had a dog bed in the background—and cried at all the artists whose lives he had changed. I told him I'd donated to the charity behind it, Artists Striving to End Poverty. He wrote back and said he'd been so moved he'd done the same.

I offered him one last Talk piece. We wouldn't have to meet. We could do it remotely. Maybe there was an upside to life temporarily without theater? All that free time in Connecticut, less deadline pressure? I was thinking it might have helped spur the Buñuel again. He declined, saying, "I really don't want any more celebration. I've been basking in it, but inundated," and ended with a P.S. that was like a lyric to the nickname I'd given our interactions: "Profile Me a Little":

"My advice is: Keep a social distance so you'll both be free."

COVID ground on through 2020 and into 2021, and I thought about Sondheim often. He was an urbane person in the old sense of the word and I didn't imagine he liked being trapped in his homes. And his living was the theater, which was closed as tightly as London's had been during the plagues. These were unprecedented times. Not that I really worried. You could live ninety years and life could still surprise you, not always in a nice way, but you kept on. You were still here.

CURTAIN

In September 2021, on *The Late Show with Stephen Colbert*, when the talk-show host, who was a long-time fan, asked Sondheim, "Are you still writing, by the way?" Sondheim said indeed he was, and that he had picked up the Buñuel again. "With any luck, we'll get it on next season," the new nonagenarian said briskly. The audience cheered. On November 15, Sondheim went to see Marianne Elliott's *Company* on Broadway. The show was playing to young and enthusiastic, mostly out-of-town audiences, almost like it was *Wicked*. When he entered, the audience and cast stood and applauded the songwriter who was bathed in a spotlight. Sondheim died just eleven days later, in Roxbury, of cardiovascular disease. Broadway dimmed its lights for a minute in his honor, and in Jersey I played *Side by Side by Sondheim* on my long-dead parents' KLH Model Twenty-Plus which had followed me from apartment to apartment to suburban home.

Sondheim and I were not in contact by then. I thought of emailing him to hear about the exciting news but never did. I assumed there would be time. I don't know how much further he ever got with the Buñuel. I'm hopeful though that one day I'll see it.

A NOTE ON THE TEXT

This book is mostly made up of the transcripts of five long conversations Stephen Sondheim and I had as we started and stopped and started on a profile on him for the *New Yorker*. The transcriptions are as accurate as I can make them. On occasion words were indistinct on the recording or I couldn't make sense of them in their context, in which case I usually made a cut rather than risk getting something wrong. One example: Sondheim at the American Museum of Natural History mentioned to me that "Somewhere Over the Rainbow" was one of his "two or three favorite American [inaudible]." But American *what?* His voice lowered, or the scribbling of my pen preempted his words at that exact moment, or an errant cough obliterated the pronouncement. I listened and listened and then my spouse and friends listened. But no one could quite pull out the word. Eventually, I gave up (though for the record I think he said "ballads").

Mostly Sondheim and I were alone but we also had a three-way conversation with Meryl Streep and a four-way one with Paul and Alexander Gemignani, father and son. In each case, I pruned the sections that principally focused on the others. Likewise, where I grew longwinded or overly auto-biographical, I trimmed myself. Sondheim was who I was there for. And on a very few occasions Sondheim made clear at the time that something he'd said would hurt someone—usually someone's family members—if it saw the light of the day, and I honored this concern posthumously by cutting the material. Sondheim could be a mean gossip but with me he rarely took pleasure in other people's misfortunes. (And, of course, the book has been reviewed by my publisher's legal department.)

Not everything anyone says is completely accurate ever. Sondheim lowered my expectations before we first met by claiming he had a "geezer memory" but I didn't find that was true at all. The composer-lyricist rarely paused as he recounted stories in detail that were forty years old. He claimed that Kaufman and Hart's version of *Merrily We Roll Along* was originally called *Americana*. Surely an error? He was conflating that play with Kaufman's *The American Way*, which came out a few years afterward. An email to an expert, Laurence Maslon at New York University, disabused me. Sondheim was basically correct about this little-known fact. *Americana* was indeed a title the authors had considered.

Even so, a fact-checker working with me identified a fair number of small flubs. I've corrected some where they were distracting but not all. The amount of money Peter Minuit paid to the original owners of Manhattan in the Rodgers and Hart song, "Give It Back to the Indians," was twenty-six dollars, not twenty-four as Sondheim sang, but this error in itself seemed at least a little interesting—that a man with such precise memory for lyrics should get one he admired slightly wrong suggested he had in fact mentally rewritten it to his greater satisfaction. Not to mention Sondheim was being faithful to the historical facts. So I left that as it was. Besides, to correct his memories seemed to me as much a betrayal of the truth of the conversation as it would have been to give him a worse memory than he had. And in the era of the internet it's easy enough to look all this up and get the correct version.

Finally, as to the larger issue of the accuracy of the dozens of stories and anecdotes Sondheim told me, I did not find any glaring errors, but it's likely not all are exactly right and certainly many are told, as most stories are, from a particular point of view. But that was itself the point: this was a conversation we were having. These are his memories. Besides, who would want a raconteur who *didn't* exaggerate sometimes? I thought that taking a mostly hands-off approach to his reminiscences, while an imperfect solution, would give readers the truest picture of what our interactions were like and also allow future scholars of musical theater a clear version of one version of the past. After that, they could head for the archives.

One final issue came up as I prepared these conversations for publication. How much to clean up the inevitable false starts and pauses of ordinary speech. Recordings capture too much and to read an exact transcript is often quite distracting. The answer I came up with was to clean things up generally but not always. You could catch the flavor of Sondheim's conversation without every *um* and *er*, though if I felt a throat clearing or a pause indicated, say, unusual uncertainty, I took the liberty of leaving it in.

ACKNOWLEDGMENTS

First and foremost I'd like to thank Jonathan Jao, my editor at Harper, who first approached me after reading at newyorker .com an excerpt from the interviews I had conducted with Sondheim, suspecting there was more. He sent me scurrying to look through three years of notes. The hunch that this could be a book proved wise. I am also grateful for the help of his assistant, David Howe, and my publicist, Tracy Locke, as well as copy editor Nora Reichard. In production, I'd like to particularly thank Lydia Weaver and Michael Siebert, and Chris Connolly in marketing. Attorney Beth Silfin is a wonder worker. Sara Nelson is a generous friend. And my deepest gratitude to Jonathan Burnham, who supported this project with enthusiasm. A thousand thanks also to my agent Elyse Cheney, and her team including Beniamino Ambrosi, the Isabels, Mendía and Kaplan, and Claire Gillespie and Grace Johnson.

Once Jonathan had alerted me to the riches in my metaphorical trunk, I turned to Alex Barasch, associate editor at the *New Yorker*, to make a first transcription and edit of the additional material, as he had of the original posting at newyorker.com. Alex's superb work was fortified by my usual amazing team of *New Yorker* talent, Daniel Zalewski, my longtime editor, who gave me the original assignment to profile the great composer-lyricist and read the book in manuscript; Michael Luo and Mike Agger of newyorker.com; Susan Morrison, who graciously asked me to write two (!) Talk pieces on Sondheim; and David Remnick, who presides wisely over us all. Emma Sargent, fresh from Karin Roffman's class on biography, fact-checked the book, getting a crash course in midcentury American musical theater in the process. Thanks also to Adam Gopnik and Anna Quindlen for interesting exchanges on Sondheim man and music.

Life is company and mine was, as ever, my spouse, Sarah Blustain (who doubles as my brilliant editor of first resort), my two children, Flora and Jules, our dog, Nemo (now happily grown mature and maybe a little mellow), and my dear friend Elizabeth Beier. My late beloved Uncle Jerry, the playwright Jerome Max, took me to my first musical and gave me my first Sondheim anecdote. Laurie Winer, longtime friend and musical theater expert, provided guidance and encouragement as she traveled around the world and finished up her own book, *Oscar Hammerstein II and the Invention of the Musical*. Cherry Provost kept me well supplied with cookies while I worked.

Additional thanks to the Guggenheim Foundation for its generous support; the Leon Levy Center for Biography for its ongoing hospitality; the Authors Guild for its strength; and PEN for its conscience.

My thanks to Paul and Alex Gemignani, and to Meryl Streep, who all graciously participated in the Talk pieces that were distilled from some of these interviews. My additional thanks to Jeff Romley, who was kind enough to accept me into his home and to give me his seat at the PEN Gala. Last, my thank-you of course to Stephen Sondheim, who was generous with his time, his thoughts, his stories, and his wisdom, who made time for me despite a pulsating deadline and a hundred revivals. If this is a story of something that didn't happen, it's at least as much of something that did. The below I offer with apologies and the hope, though, God knows, not the expectation, that Steve would have found it funny:

Profile me a little
Ask me just enough.
Pry, but not too deeply.
Judge, but not too rough.
I'll give you wine and seltzer
Lots of breaks to pee
That's the way it ought to be.
I'm ready!